Reviews for Previous Versions

☆☆☆☆☆
5.0 out of 5 stars

This book will revolutionize how you view the power of marketing and social media

By Jeff Stodola

A definite must-read for everybody in the aviation business! Tons of great information and ideas about how to create a comprehensive and long term marketing plan using social media.

☆☆☆☆☆
5.0 out of 5 stars

A warning... you'll need a pen and paper while you're reading this book to write down specific things you need to do for your business.

Full disclosure: I've worked with ABCI in the past and am probably biased toward their strategies since I know how well they work.

Unsolicited Review - This is totally worth the few hours of reading time.

By Jerry Buccola on Amazon

Read this on the flight to national NBAA convention. This book is worth the few hours of reading time because it is REALLY helpful. Why? It is packed with concrete practical analysis, tips, and recommendations on implementing an effective social media presence. Highlights for me: 1) The fighter pilot checklist of Observe/Orient/Decide/Act, 2) Why Content Matters - with a half dozen effective items to include in postings, 3) LinkedIn Success Stories, 4) Why Google Plus is Worth Evaluating.

Read it. I mean it.

By the way, this is an unsolicited review.

Digital Marketing Guide
for
Aviation Professionals

2020 Edition

ISBN- 978-0-578-51169-6

ABCI books are available for special promotions and premiums. For details, contact ABCI at 702-987-1679 or email books@aviationbusinessconsultants.com

Revised but previously published as "The Down to Earth Social Media Guide to High Altitude Results" in 2015.

To our members and clients, who generously
share their data with us and with each other
for the overall success of the aviation industry.

Table of Contents

Social media replaces nothing,

But compliments everything.

- Neal Schaffer

Foreword to the Social Media Guide for Aviation Professionals

By Kim Walsh-Phillips

I'm pleased to write this foreword because John and Paula Williams and I share a passion for bringing traditional marketing disciplines of well-planned campaigns and disciplined measurement to a medium that's gotten a bad rap, particularly in business-to-business and high-ticket sales as a "random act of marketing."

Social media is usually overhyped, or underrated, but seldom seen for what it is – a powerful marketing tool.

In my first book, the *No BS Guide to Direct Response Social Media Marketing*, (co-written with Dan S. Kennedy) our challenge was to literally "write the book" on social media with a famously skeptical co-author for a famously skeptical audience – savvy business owners who have gobbled up ascerbic, non-nonsense (No B.S.!) titles on such traditional topics as pricing, sales, and ruthless people management.

Much of my digital marketing practice is focused on financial industry professionals, who can be almost as skeptical and traditional as . . . shall we say, aviation industry professionals!

The No BS Social Media book, and my latest book, *The Ultimate Guide to Instagram for Business*, were tremendously successful because of my fabulously humorous yet informative writing, and also because of the profound need for credible information by serious professionals.

The Social Media Guide for Aviation Professionals lends some much-needed specificity and reassurance about how to use these tools successfully to target decision-makers in this unique industry.

Kim Walsh-Philips is an award-winning speaker, author, podcaster and CEO of three sperate companies – Elite Digital Group, a direct-response social media agency, Elite Capital Advisers, a lead generation firm for financial advisers, and Powerful Professionals, an association where influence and success meet. Kim has brought in more than a billion dollars online with her laser focus on increasing revenue through direct-response marketing. She is also the co-author of the *No B.S. Guide to Direct Response Social Media Marketing*.

Introduction to the 2020 Edition

Writing any book about something as ephemeral as digital marketing is taking a huge risk.

Four years in digital marketing is a LONG TIME. It's also not as significant as you might think. We all have the same concerns AND the same aspirations for digital marketing – privacy concerns, effectiveness, and return on investment.

Many people who had privacy concerns in 2015 have had those concerns overwhelmed by the business case for inexpensive, responsive advertising and customer service tools.

There were still companies in 2015 who thought they could simply "opt out" of digital marketing an online media altogether. They'd done business for years by word of mouth, so why change now?

What's changed is that it's no longer just the "young folks," (I say as I reach for my reading glasses.) The landscape and culture for all of us have been shaped by social media.

Many smart companies have incorporated guidelines in their employee manuals about making the company look bad or divulging the "secret recipes" online AND offline, recognizing that an employee could make your company look bad by saying something he shouldn't in a public restaurant on his day off.

It's smart to have standards of behavior and to hire carefully, now more than ever.

In terms of effectiveness, there has been much talk about "ad saturation" in some of the online media, particularly Facebook, as it changes its algorithm to keep users happy and engaged and repeated calls to "show fewer ads."

Facebook has responded by raising the prices and standards for advertising, allowing a smaller percentage of text in each image, for example. And an ad that used to reach a very specific target for mere pennies now costs a dime or so – a significant change by percentage, but still a much lower cost-per-impression than most other advertising venues.

In terms of return on investment, all of the digital marketing opportunities competing with one another has been great for advertisers, particularly in the aviation industry where our markets tend to be geographically diverse but still very small. We can target everyone who has an interest in the KingAir 350 ER, from India to Africa to Alaska, sitting at our desks and clicking a few buttons.

The field has also broadened, which is why we've changed the name. A good digital marketing strategy should consider social media, to be sure, but it should also include retargeting, SEO, pay-per-click, and other online marketing tools and techniques in an integrated marketing system.

Considering social media in a vacuum, or just assigning it to a junior person at your firm to "handle that" is as irresponsible as putting an intern in charge of your front office and all customer interactions!

So, here's what's changed in this edition of our Guide:

We changed the name.

We've added

- Updated Social Media Survey Results
- Six Prospecting Tips for Using Social Media
- Quick Tip for Getting More Reviews
- Digital Marketing -Enjoy Responsibly
- What's the Best Advertising Media for Reaching Aviation Consumers and Companies?
- Digital vs. Print -Round Two (Ding!)
- Digital Marketing Glossary
- Social Media Habits of Highly Successful Salespeople

Fear and Loathing of Marketing Tools

Dan S Kennedy, a well-known marketing authority, is almost equally well known for his distaste for all things digital – smart phones, social media, and the Internet in general.

While he has professionally profited from using these marketing tools, he says "If I could get the powers that be to put that back into Pandora's Box, I'd happily give the money back. But since that isn't going to happen, my personal loathing for these things is irrelevant."

While I am equally irritated by texting drivers and inane celebrity-stalking and family fights gone rapidly and spectacularly public via social media, and in spite of my respect for Mr. Kennedy (we are involved with his Peak Performers mastermind group and travel to meet with them several days each year.) I have to ask – **how can you loathe a tool?**

I once dropped a heavy socket wrench on my toe. Yes, I was barefoot in the garage working on something, and yes, I know that wasn't my brightest move. But still, my big toenail turned black, fell off, and took months to grow back.

I was not happy with this at all.

But do I loathe socket wrenches?

No.

It is merely a tool that I unwisely misused and hurt myself with.

John gallantly threatened to throw it out. (He has also said he will throw away any kitchen knife that I cut myself with.)

But we both know the truth.

Facebook, Twitter, LinkedIn, YouTube and other forums, websites and channels are all simply that – marketing tools to be used for specific tasks. They can be used for good or evil. They should be handled intelligently.

Our suggestions –

- **Designate one person** to field comments, complaints and compliments that come in via your website, social media or other online channels.

- Make sure they know the **limits of their discretion** and what types of topics should be escalated. (Don't feed the trolls!)

- Create an editorial calendar for your website and social media publishing. Be proactive rather than reactive.

- Set up **social media guidelines** for employees. Let them know that gossip and/or defamation in any context, whether at a cocktail party or online, is not acceptable behavior. Include an online communication plan in your disaster recovery planning.

- Draft some **generic messaging** for likely scenarios so that you can "fill in the blanks" with specific details if you ever have a need to communicate quickly. (I.e. A flight school might draft announcements regarding safety incidents, security breaches, aircraft mechanical problems, etc.) "Better to have it and never need it than to need it and not have it," as the cliche goes.

- **Never work in the garage barefoo**t.

A little common sense is necessary when working with heavy or powerful tools.

Social Media Survey Results – Mythbusting!

- "Social media is only used by kids and salespeople."

- "Maybe you can sell retail products like games and music downloads on social media, but it's of no use for complex or business to business sales."

- "An occasional marketing message on social media every once in awhile is plenty."

Our Social Media Survey Results report busts these myths – at least for aviation professionals.

We asked aviation professionals which social media channels they personally use most often, as well as which channels they use for marketing.

We provide the complete results to our clients and members, but here's a summary of some of the highlights.

Who Responded to Our Survey?

A fairly wide cross section of aviation companies responded to the survey, including a large number of aviation training organizations, aviation consultants, B2B (Business to Business) service providers, B2B product manufacturers, FBOs, Airport Authorities, MROs, Charter Organizations and Aviation Product Retailers.

This belies the myth that only B2C (Business to Consumer) marketing professionals are interested in social media.

1. Which of the following best describes your company?

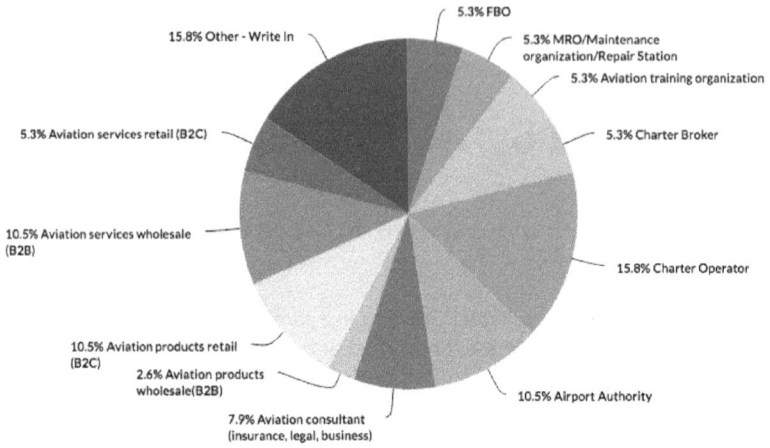

5.3% FBO

5.3% MRO/Maintenance organization/Repair Station

15.8% Other - Write In

5.3% Aviation training organization

5.3% Charter Broker

5.3% Aviation services retail (B2C)

5.3% Charter Broker

10.5% Aviation services wholesale (B2B)

15.8% Charter Operator

10.5% Aviation products retail (B2C)

2.6% Aviation products wholesale(B2B)

10.5% Airport Authority

7.9% Aviation consultant (insurance, legal, business)

The next question asked about the respondent's position in the company. Again, we received a large number of responses from founders and C-Level executives. This contradicts the stereotype that social media is for lower-level executives, operatives and salespeople.

2. Which of the following best describes your role?

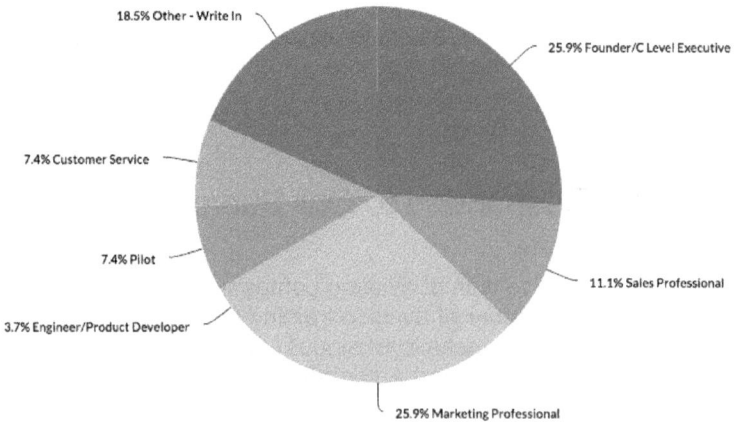

18.5% Other - Write In

25.9% Founder/C Level Executive

7.4% Customer Service

7.4% Pilot

11.1% Sales Professional

3.7% Engineer/Product Developer

25.9% Marketing Professional

How often do you access any Social Media Channel?

Last year, we were surprised to find that 50% of our respondents used social media more than once a day. Apparently, that trend is continuing, with 58% of respondents reporting use of some social media channels more than once per day. Infrequent users are also decreasing.

3. How often do you log into any social media network (e.g. Facebook, LinkedIn, Google+, Twitter, Pinterest, Instagram, Youtube, etc.?)

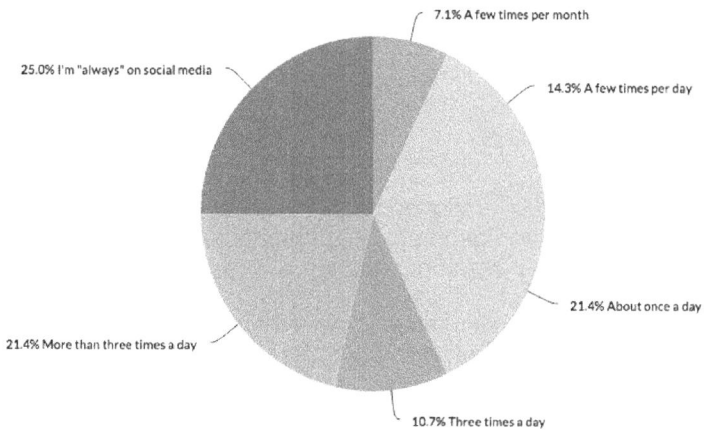

- 7.1% A few times per month
- 25.0% I'm "always" on social media
- 14.3% A few times per day
- 21.4% About once a day
- 21.4% More than three times a day
- 10.7% Three times a day

For more detail, we asked respondents to report how often they used each of these channels.

- The most frequently accessed channels were LinkedIn, Facebook, Youtube, and Twitter.
- Google Plus, Pinterest, Instagram, and Reddit were used far less frequently.
- If you sell a product or service to aviation professionals, this is where your customers are spending their time:

4. Which social media networking site to personally access most often?

	Not at All	Seldom	Monthly	Multiple Times a Month	Weekly	Multiple Times a Week	Daily	Multiple Times a Day
LinkedIn	2 8.3%	2 8.3%	2 8.3%	1 4.2%	3 12.5%	4 16.7%	5 20.8%	5 20.8%
Facebook	2 9.1%	1 4.5%	0 0.0%	0 0.0%	2 9.1%	0 0.0%	7 31.8%	10 45.5%
Twitter	6 25.0%	3 12.5%	1 4.2%	1 4.2%	1 4.2%	1 4.2%	7 29.2%	4 16.7%
YouTube	2 8.3%	1 4.2%	2 8.3%	5 20.8%	3 12.5%	5 20.8%	4 16.7%	2 8.3%
Google+	7 28.0%	0 0.0%	1 4.0%	3 12.0%	6 24.0%	3 12.0%	3 12.0%	2 8.0%
Instagram	8 33.3%	0 0.0%	3 12.5%	3 12.5%	4 16.7%	2 8.3%	2 8.3%	2 8.3%
Pinterest	9 36.0%	1 4.0%	4 16.0%	4 16.0%	3 12.0%	3 12.0%	0 0.0%	1 4.0%
Reddit	11 50.0%	2 9.1%	4 18.2%	2 9.1%	0 0.0%	1 4.5%	1 4.5%	1 4.5%

We asked how often respondent used these channels for advertising. There is a still a large gap between personal use and marketing use. . . which to us, looks like an opportunity!

Your customers are using social media personally, but your competitors are not using it to market their products. . . Hmmm. . .

5. How often does your company or organization use social media for marketing, PR, or customer service?

	Not at all	Seldom	Monthly	Multiple times a month	Weekly	Multiple Times a Week	Daily	Multiple Times a Day
Facebook	0 0.0%	5 19.2%	2 7.7%	0 0.0%	0 0.0%	3 11.5%	8 30.8%	8 30.8%
Twitter	5 18.5%	0 0.0%	3 11.1%	0 0.0%	2 7.4%	5 18.5%	8 29.6%	4 14.8%
LinkedIn	4 16.0%	4 16.0%	0 0.0%	4 16.0%	0 0.0%	0 0.0%	7 28.0%	6 24.0%
Google+	10 38.5%	2 7.7%	4 15.4%	2 7.7%	4 15.4%	1 3.8%	1 3.8%	2 7.7%
Instagram	8 32.0%	1 4.0%	2 8.0%	2 8.0%	3 12.0%	5 20.0%	1 4.0%	3 12.0%
Pinterest	11 42.3%	3 11.5%	4 15.4%	4 15.4%	2 7.7%	0 0.0%	0 0.0%	2 7.7%

Conclusions – What Did We Learn from the 2019 Survey?

Social media has become a part of the fabric of life. The individual tools ebb and flow, but usage in general has increased overall. (Or perhaps, people are finally ADMITTING to use it because there it's more generally accepted among professionals.)

In 2014, many of the comments in the survey were derogatory about social media or about the respondents' own use of it. "I don't really use social media, I only use LinkedIn." (Reminds me of a "vegan" I sat next to on an airplane that only eats grass-fed, pastured beef.) Or "I only created an account so I could talk to my kids/grandkids."

I know one senior aviation company executive who found an interesting article via Facebook several years ago. He wanted to share it with a colleague, but didn't want to simply share it because he felt his colleague would know he had been "wasting time on Facebook." I showed him how to get the "raw link" of the original article so that he could send it in an email.

We laughed recently about how careful he had been. "Now I just click the 'share' button. Everybody's on Facebook anyway and nobody thinks a thing of it."

Now people are much more accepting of their own use and that of their employees and team members.

When we first ran this survey in 2014, we did not think to include the category of "more than once per day" for any social media. Who does that?

But the prevalence of mobile devices, the ease of use of social media, and the changes to our daily habits of how we interact, even with our own friends and family have changed significantly over the last four years.

What does this mean for aviation sales and marketing professionals?

- More of your customers are on social media, more of the time.
- It's become "socially acceptable" for even the most serious, senior aviation professionals and high net worth individuals to come "out of the closet" and admit their usage publicly, and to share items they find on social media with colleagues.
- Many admit that they respond to ads
- Facebook, Twitter, LinkedIn and YouTube are still the "big four," with others such as Instagram, Pinterest and others trailing behind.

Note – Google's parent company Alphabet has announced that Google Plus will be discontinued this year, so we'll be dropping it from our surveys and most other reporting.

Direct Response Social Media – An Interview with Kim Walsh-Phillips

This is our first of, hopefully many, celebrity author interviews! We're talking with the author of a the best-selling book on direct response social media.

We were thrilled to get Kim Walsh-Phillips to spend some time using her social media expertise. Kim gives us some specific tips that are perfect for the complex, high-trust, large-ticket and long-cycle sales that the aviation industry is famous (or infamous) for.

Kim, @KWalshPhillips, is the award-winning Speaker, Author, Podcaster and CEO of Elite Digital Group, a direct-response social media agency. Kim has brought in more than a billion dollars through her clients with her laser focus on increasing their revenue through direct-response marketing. She is author of "No B.S. Guide to Direct Response Social Media Marketing: The Ultimate No Holds Barred Guide to Producing Measurable, Monetizable Results with Social Media Marketing," with Dan Kennedy. Kim also leads the top-ranked podcast, "Facebook Sales Strategies," on iTunes. She resides with her very tall husband, who is often asked to get things down from the ridiculously tall cabinets in their house, and their two glitter-and-all-things-pink-obsessed daughters, Bella and Katie, just outside of NYC.

SOCIAL MEDIA MARKETING IN AVIATION

A Discussion of "No BS" Strategies for
Aviation Sales and Marketing Pros

Paula Anderson Williams
Aviation Marketing Specialist

Kim Walsh-Phillips,
Social Media Marketing Specialist

Transcript – Interview with Kim Walsh-Phillips

Paula Williams: Kim, I'm just really excited that you're spending some time with us today. I know we have a really nichy audience, which is the aviation professionals sales and marketing professionals, and we love your book.

We've been reading it in our book club.

Kim Walsh-Phillips: Thank you.

Paula Williams: One of our favorite so far. So people tend to think that social media and Facebook, in particular, is somehow separate from the general rules of marketing. In your book, you make a special point about noting that the six basics of effective marketing still apply even though we may be using social media, which is new.

Can you tell us more about this?

Kim Walsh-Phillips: Absolutely, so there are six things that really can apply to any type of marketing, and I think that's what's so important. People get onto social and they feel like it's a different place, it's different a different beast, but social media is not marketing.

And so you want to apply great marketing tactics, so these six tactics could really be applied to any marketing strategy, but we'll talk about specifically social for the purposes of today's call. So you want to have a plan, number one, to sell from the very beginning. I cannot tell you how many clients come to work with my firm, and they have been utilizing social media, but never realize how they're going to sell.

Paula Williams: Wow.

Kim Walsh-Phillips: Never want to come across, yeah, sorry, go ahead?

Paula Williams: I just said wow. It's amazing to me that somebody would be doing marketing with no endgame.

Kim Walsh-Phillips: Exactly, it's incredible because you can't have an ROI if you don't plan for it. I mean, you'd never want to come across as the used car salesman, balancing on his next skill.

But you do need to ensure you give your prospects a consistent opportunity to connect and do business with you. So before you start doing your next post or your next ad, plan out how those ads and posts are going to turn into a sale. And what I recommend is you actually start from the backwards, to the front.

So you first determine what is going to be our offer to get them into a conversation with us. And then how can we drive content to that offer, and then how can we begin to attract the right prospects to us? So you can begin with the end in mind.

Number two, you always want to make sure that you're giving some time sensitive offer, you don't ever want to make delaying a desirable option. I mean, automation's possible, right? You could set up your offers, and you could just let them run forever, but your offers really need to be fresh, new, and ever-changing with clear deadlines.

I mean, one of the people that we look and respect to, Dane Kennedy, he talks about all the time, how Tide literally changes its packaging or its feature or its scent. Every single month, they offered something new, not because the product doesn't work, but because people get bored.

They want something different, they need something that's going to drive their action right now. Do the same thing with your marketing, and make it time sensitive cuz if it's not, it's going to go onto the do it later list. And if it's on your do it later list, they're never going to do, right, we have too many things that we need to get done today.

And along those lines, give them very, very clear instructions on what you want them to do right now. You want your audience to click over to your website? Tell them that, click on this link and now, go to the top of the page, read it, fill out the form below it.

It sounds ridiculous If you split test this telling them versus not telling them, I'll be willing to bet you the clear instructions will win every single time. People want to be told what to do. Number four, there will be tracking and measurement, you'll never know your ROI in social media marketing unless you track it.

We have a lot of fun at my company, but [LAUGH] so I always say my number one thing is In God We Trust, everyone else bring data. [LAUGH] Okay.

Paula Williams: Right.

Kim Walsh-Phillips: You need to be able to measure, and if anyone, any marketer, any digital professional, every marketing staff person, if they ever tell you, we can't measure that, I don't know how well this did, I'm not sure what this is doing for us.

Do not work with them anymore until they can because everything you do on social media can be tracked and measured, and only if they can, should you be engaging into it. Very, very, very important because results rule period. So number five is results rule period. You should only be scaling up your marketing up or down if you are seeing the results that work.

And so what we recommend is you start very, very small. You begin to scale up and only when you see things work, do you engage in them. Gary Vaynerchuk is very popular when it comes to social media, that I really, I'm cautious about the advice that he gives.

Cuz I find it to work really well for a big marketing, big companies, huge marketing budget and can throw money at a lot of different channels. I don't love his philosophy of trying the newest media or getting ahead of the curve, because what you're doing is you're spending a lot of time and energy going into uncharted waters and trying to see if you get an ROI.

Believe that you should spend your time in the social media channels that we already know, are going to produce the results that you're looking for. And then the final rule for marketing is that branding should be a by-product of effective direct response marketing, not the other way around, so branding is great, okay?

You want to make sure your brand's consistent, every social media page looks the same, has the right colors, your messaging is on point. You're always putting across that one big idea you want to be known for as a company. Maybe what you're excellent at is customer service or maybe it's the ongoing relationships with your clients, or that you're able to get your customers the most cutting edge technology when it comes to making their aviation purchase.

But you still have to get at some point for them to do something, whether it's give you a review, give you a referral, provide an email address to you, get on the phone to have a conversation. There needs to be a plan of how that engagement and awareness is going to turn into a conversation about sales, or else, you shouldn't be on there in the first place.

Paula Williams: That makes perfect sense, and that ties in really well, ABCI does a social media survey of aviation sales and marketing professionals. So if you can look at where are your competitors and where are your prospective customers already spending time, that really ties in especially to that 0.5.

So I'm glad you've mentioned that, and that's so important not to just be chasing the latest shiny object.

Kim Walsh-Phillips: Yeah, it could be so tempting, right, cuz as marketers, as sales professionals, as entrepreneurs, business owners, we are very much enticed by shiny objects. [LAUGH]

Paula Williams: Right.

Kim Walsh-Phillips: It's hard to stay on point, but yeah, with a plan in place, it becomes much easier

Paula Williams: Fantastic, so let's talk about Facebook as a research tool. The demographics of our insiders, target customers, are generally 45 plus, males, 16 plus, caught up years of college. Higher than average instances of military experience, average income of 75K, and they drive 4 year old cars, right? So I found all this out using a technique that you demonstrated at a GKIC event last year that just absolutely blew me away.

It's in the Audience Insights section of Facebook. Can you talk a little bit more about Audience Insights and some of that fantastically scary research that you can do?

Kim Walsh-Phillips: Yeah, sure, so it has been for a long time, since there was direct mail, that large companies could purchase lists of people based on their behaviors.

The whole business behind Publishers Clearing House Sweepstakes is really just a lead generation company, and they've been doing that for a very long time. And big companies like Comcast or Bank of America have been able to purchase that data cuz they have to buy these lists of at 100,000 people.

Well, all of that data that those companies buy is generally coming from credit card information. When you make a purchase with your credit card, it's not just showing up on your transaction report, when you look online or on the paper payment or bill statement. It is also being sold to data mining companies, unless you opt out of it which very, very few, I think, it's actually 1% of people do.

Paula Williams: Right.

Kim Walsh-Phillips: Yeah, so when you make a purchase, everything is tracked from, I just bought this specific book, I like to buy Yoplait yogurt. Or there's a television show that I like, all of that is being tracked about me, and it's being sold. Now, again as consumers, we can find that incredibly creepy, right?

But as a marketer, it's amazingly effective because now we're not just throwing the spaghetti at the wall and seeing what sticks, we are able to pinpoint our exact message on our exact prospect. Okay, because we can now access this data inside of Facebook. Facebook has partnered with data mining companies, Axie, an example of one, that polls information from credit cards, and now you can pull the exact person that you are looking to reach.

So yes, you can poll people based on their education, what kind of car they drive? How long they have been married? What aged children do they have? What's their net worth? What are their are interests? What is their purchasing behaviors? What's amazing is that you could even, we just saw this facet today, you can even find someone who is traveling to somewhere.

So how would you use that, yeah, if you're going to a conference, and let's say you were going to attend an event. And this is one of my favorite strategies, so let's say you're going to go to some networking event or a conference or an expo. Whatever you're going to attend, prior to attending, maybe you want to be established as an authority.

Now you don't even need to be an exhibitor at that event. Maybe you're going to be networking at that event, and you want people there to already know who you are and perceive you as a celebrity or industry expert. You could simply take one of your blog posts, create an ad for it or a post, and you promote the post.

And you promote the post to people who are fans of the organization who is putting on that event. So let's say you are going to go to a travel, let's say, Robb Report is going to have a big travel expo, so you are going to a Robb Report travel event.

And you would target Robb Report, and then you would target people who were traveling to the exact location you were visiting. And then you could geo target the ad, so it would only show to them the area that you were targeting, okay.

Paula Williams: That's fantastic. That is so cool.

Kim Walsh-Phillips: I know, right? So you're not wasting money going after a million different people, you're actually only targeting the people that you're looking at. Now, it goes even in a level of, this is even creepier, but again, this stays amongst us as marketers. Businesses can now buy, it's called a beacon or get a beacon from Facebook.

Now, a beacon is a device that tracks the mobile phone of Facebook users, okay? And so if somebody saw your ad, and the facility has a beacon, you will know if the person who saw your ad actually went to the place where you were targeting, okay. Physical, actual location, so if you were targeting, let's say there's an Expo Hall again on targeting people where travels at Expo Hall that are fans of it.

I will be able to tell if those people actually were at the event, and saw my ad, or how many of them did.

Paula Williams: That's fantastic. See, the world's largest aviation trade show, is in Orlando in November. So everybody who is going to the NBAA convention in Orlando in November, should be listening to this, and taking notes, because this is just gold.

Kim Walsh-Phillips: Yeah, and I mean, you could do the same thing with targeting employers, so let's say there's a certain individual that makes sense for you, so we're talking about let's say maybe your profile. Again, if you're going to say 16 years of college, higher than average, this is a military experience.

Average incomes, so maybe we're going to put in there, we want $75,000 income. We could say, that they had military in there, and maybe there's a major employer in our area that would make sense to target. You can target that employer ahead of time or if you're trying to work out a great deal with somebody, I've done that for, if I want to become a guest columnist in a publication, I've targeted the employees of that publication-

Paula Williams: Wow.

Kim Walsh-Phillips: Prior to pitching them, yeah. So Ink Magazine and Forbes, prior to having conversations with them, they were seeing my content online because I was targeting their employees.

Paula Williams: That's fantastic. Yeah, that's really, really great and really usable too. What are the misconceptions, I think that happens especially in aviation is that our customers are sometimes very, very tiny, tiny niche less.

Because we sell high end, complex products usually in a business-to-business situation. So we have very, very specific client list, and one of our clients has a potential market as an example of 67 people. Now there's a misconception that you have to have thousands and thousands to make Facebook advertising work to you.

But how can someone like this with a teeny tiny universe of prospective buyers, leverage Facebook?

Kim Walsh-Phillips: Sure, so what I would say, I mean if you're talking with a list that small, you can obviously get the contact information for all of your prospects. And then you can upload that list to Facebook, and you can actually target them.

As long as your list is over 20 people, you can target it. And what I would be saying in that situation is you don't need them to opt into anything because you can get their contact information. I would be using that as an opportunity to position yourself as an authority or expert.

Again, so they are seeing your contents at the same time where you're doing your phone calls and outreach. So if I was going to do that I would say, okay, we're going to do a FedEx direct mail campaign. We're going to send some shock and awe, and it's going to be followed up by a phone call the afternoon of the morning that they get my shock and awe package.

And I might say I'm going to do that over the course of three days. Two weeks to prior to doing that direct mail, I would be making sure that they were seeing my content ahead of time because Facebook can be use as a nurture campaign. So perhaps you tell stories on day one through three, you're going to see a post about a success story you've had with one of your customers.

And days five to seven, maybe it's an article that you wrote, maybe eight through ten, it's another success story. And you're showing them all of that content as though you were emailing them, but you're not because your position's on Facebook. So that way you're the authority cuz now you have an article, and experts are great things, and so you're now an author.

I would be seeding my market ahead of my big mail campaign or ahead of my outreach program by using Facebook as my resource.

Paula Williams: That's fantastic. That actually is a really wonderful a campaign idea, that kinda goes step by step. I know a lot of the folks that have been using Facebook in the past, at least myself personally anyway, have sometimes done good things accidentally on Facebook because it's new and because we're experimenting and things like that, but that really makes it methodical.

Kim Walsh-Phillips: Yeah, and having a system in place, then we're doing things because they're important instead of urgent. It's much easier to follow. It also gives you a baseline because then now we can say, okay, this step worked, but this one should be tweaked. So systematizing ahead of time of course will help you to scale your results very quickly.

Paula Williams: Right, that's fantastic. We did have a client that sold a business jet from a contact that originated from a Facebook post. So I know in a lot of cases, people think of Facebook as business to consumer marketing and also maybe the smaller retail products. But can you tell us more about how you could use Facebook as small steps to a larger sale?

Kim Walsh-Phillips: Sure, so yeah, when you're building out your Facebook campaign and you're going to a large scale sale, you want to again think about it as a, how would I build that relationship out? Similar to dating, really, you're dating your prospect, to turn it into a conversation, that first date, to turn to another conversation, eventually to ask them to marry you or to make the purchase.

So step one, what would you want them to think about you if they saw you from across the room, right? So how do you want your profile set up, in a way that establishes yourself as an expert? What kind of content do you want to provide? What social proof can you show?

These are all the things you're setting up to your house before you invite them in. And then you begin to share content that's incredibly valuable to them, establishes you as the authority or expert, it's always step one. Step two is to ask for their contact information because, you want to own that.

You don't want Facebook to be the only place where you talk to them because, then if something happens to Facebook, either the company itself or they kick you off, let's say, you never want to make that your only channel. Plus, why keep paying Facebook to contact someone when you contact them for free if they're on your email list or a direct mail list.

So get their contact information by offering an incentive that works. As another tip on that one, never make you offer for the first time on Facebook, right? Why do I say this, right? Because then you're testing Facebook and the offer at the same time. And that does not work because you don't know which piece is working and which isn't.

So I suggest you always, always test if it's an offer, if it's an lead magnet. First, if you have an email list, with your email list. If you don't have that, if you're simply starting out, then reach out to a couple people that you know and send it to them, personally and see if they respond to it, at least to be interested enough to opt in.

Or contact some people you know on LinkedIn, and say, I'm not telling you anything, I just want to check out before I post this [INAUDIBLE] online, would you be one to take a look at this? And get some feedback. Always research it prior to putting it online because you can't pull apart.

You can't optimize a Facebook campaign if you're running an offer that you don't know works. I'll give you an example, so it's for a different niche, but it's a client who we got, it was a high end product, 62 people raised their hand online. And said that they would be interested in purchasing this product.

62 people, nobody actually did, none of them, but they, come to find out, they had never even though we had gotten different information, they had never tested this before. And now we don't know what was wrong, right? I can't say it was Facebook because I don't know if the offer ever would have converted.

So then we got into their email, and we tested the offer, and then nobody of the thousands of people on their list took advantage of it. So it was not Facebook, right? It was the offer, and so now we know, now they're testing a bunch of offers with their list first.

And then we'll go back into Facebook cuz we know we had the right targeting, we had people who had raised their hands, we just didn't have an offer that would convert. So then we can separate each step and optimize it if you do it that way.

Paula Williams: Right, that's one of the problems that we have in the aviation industry, is that we have such small audiences that it's hard to do really good testing.

But one thing that you can do, is reach out to the other members of the insider's circle, because they're really, really good at picking each other's stuff apart [LAUGH] in a friendly way before you go spend money on something. So that would work really well before you did an offer on a Facebook or other social media advertising.

So that's fantastic. Let's talk about some of the services that you offer that might be particularly interesting to aviation sales and marketing professionals.

Kim Walsh-Phillips: Well, sure, so what our sweet spot is is showing people how to do this themselves, effectively, doing it with them, or doing it for them.

So what does that mean? We have programs that show you how to set up an effective Facebook campaign funnel, utilize that along with LinkedIn, Twitter, Instagram, utilize social media channels to get in ROI. A few workshops where we will do with you just brand one of those last week, it had several companies attend.

And they were able to fully launch their campaigns and bring these in the door before they left. Then the final piece, which is how most companies utilize my firm is that we'll actually go into whatever funnel you have now, not inside of social media. And create a social media compliant and effective campaign, so we are able to utilize social media to drive people to see you as the authority and expert, give you their contact information, and then become a sales conversation.

That's what we're focused on, not the fluffiness of clicks or likes or no, those things are important, but only if they are producing ROI, so our campaigns are completely ROI and metric focused.

Paula Williams: Fantastic, that makes perfect sense, and once again, I know our group is really loving your book.

And anybody who's listening to this who may want a nice introduction, we highly, highly recommend the book, and you can find that on Amazon. Unless there is someplace you'd prefer to have people go find that?

Kim Walsh-Phillips: No, that's great. If they just want to check out a free chapter of the book, you can go to nobschapter.com.

And The No BS social media book, we'll give you lots of bonuses and perks, but you'll see that link inside the book itself. So Amazon is fine, or you can get a sneak peek at No BS Chapter. And, Paula, so that we make sure that the folks come through to you, to contact us.

I think, it probably would make sense if they are interested in talking to us further about product program services maybe go through you? Do it that way?

Paula Williams: Absolutely, yeah. We'll certainly put links on the transcript of this podcast on our website. And we'll also be sharing some information in the insider circle about how better to take advantage of some of the things that we talked about today.

Paula Williams: Yeah, I think that would be wonderful, so you could make those introductions and connections that work for everyone.

So thank you so much for joining us. I really enjoyed the conversation, and I look forward to seeing what people do with their social media in aviation. I hope this is going to be a really evolving thing over the next couple of years. I think it's long overdue for aviation.

Kim Walsh-Phillips: Thank you so much for having me, it's a complete pleasure.

Transcript – Book Club Conversation – No BS Social Media Marketing

Paula Williams: People tend to think that social media is magical or different than marketing in general but it is really not. It follows the same basic rules of all marketing. So, if any of you guys have any thoughts about that or any comments.

MARKETING MONDAY

Book Club Discussion

John Williams: That sounds like that was written in my marketing class and Business School

Paula Williams: Really, I thought your marketing course in business school was a little bit less than direct response.

John Williams: Well, no, but I'm using the sort of generically. She was of the opinion that if anybody brought anything they had to be marketed to first. Otherwise there's always an offer.

A reason to respond, and so forth. I had many long and interesting discussions with her about that.

Paula Williams: Right. I think of the things that happen in aviation. One of the things that happens the least or the one that gets done the least is number 2. There will always be a reason to respond right now.

A lot of times we'll see ads in aviation magazines and other kinds of things that they introduce a product and say, here it is, end of story. And there's no offer really or certainly no reason to respond right now. And if that's the case I think it gets put on a in our stack of things to do later and then it never gets done right?

John Williams: Yes.

Kathryn Creedy

- Communication Strategies
- KathrynBCreedy.com
- KCreedy@Gmail.com

Kathryn Creedy: If you want to see really good reason to respond right now, we've all seen the infomercials, late night infomercials. And they say, but wait! If you order now, you get the Ginsu knives! That's the kind of response that you wanna get.

Paula Williams: Right and the other thing is a lot of time we are selling really complex or high value items.

Like, Gene, you're selling airplanes, and people aren't going to respond right now to buy an airplane. It takes a certain amount of time, so if you give people a reason to respond right now, it might be for a consultation or a report or any number and things like that.

I know we've tried these things with you.

Gene Clow

GREAT CIRCLE
AIRCRAFT

Sales, Acquisitions &
Consulting in the NorthWest

- Great Circle Aircraft
- GreatCircleAircraft.com
- GClow@GCAircraft.com

Gene Clow: Yeah, no I've never had that phone call on Monday morning where someone called and said, "I need it and I need it today!"

Paula Williams: [LAUGH]

Gene Clow: In fact, I've still a couple more years to go, don't give up yet.

Paula Williams: There you go. And those are not exactly impulse purchases. This is not candy at the checkout stands. [LAUGH]

Gene Clow: And it quite honestly when I they used to run ads that had a minimal response. And they referred to those as "positioning advertisements" more so than a desire to get a response of some sort. You know for all I know they may have been trying to support the publication at the same time.

Paula Williams: Right, they might be, and honestly there's no reason that you can't do positioning and still have a call to action in that ad. Running an ad that has a response mechanism, and that is measured and is followed up after and all of those things, still positions you, right?

It says all of those things that you wanna do for branding, it doesn't really detract from positioning. What do you think, John?

John Williams: Well-

Paula Williams: [LAUGH].

John Williams: My Marketing Professor said, that what Gene said, basically, positioning is expensive. We had a software program that we used called Markstrat.

Which you did all these various things and you had through my and through my that and see which one worked the best. And then all this testing over some number, some amount of time. Then you went back and said, okay, this is what I want. Put all the remaining dollars here.

Well, that's nice if you've got $800,000 which we were playing with. But how many people have that? You can't afford to do that. This is a better way.

Paula Williams: I think that a lot of those university classes are assuming that your Nike or that your advertising for Coke.

You're put on one of those large accounts for a Fortune 50 companies which is great. Even so I think I think everybody would do better, especially smaller companies, if every ad serves more than one purpose. And if they follow at least five of these six rules that there's no reason why they can't do all six, right?

John Williams: Well if you're not just throwing money away.

Paula Williams: Right, right, exactly. And I don't know if Jeff is on the call, Jeff Stodola?

John Williams: No.

Paula Williams: I thought I heard, okay he does when he does his test flights, marketing test flights, a call to action is really what he's looking for and I know he's got his own version of this.

Where he's looking for, is this ad likely to be successful and these are the factors that he's likely to be looking into. So, that is cool. All right, next thing. Okay, nine lead magnet examples. In our lead magnets, one of our lead magnet is a list of 17 lead magnets.

[LAUGH] So we have some different ones but these are the ones that Kim wants included in her book. And a lot of these are different. They're not things that I would have thought of, so this is cool. Anybody tried any of these or thought about any of these?

John Williams: Well, we've tried a couple.

Paula Williams: I think we've tried, we've done a guide, we've done a blueprint, we've done a checklist, we've done an eBook and we've done webinar registration, so we've done five of the nine.

Paula Williams: Of them, one of the things that I'd suggest is that the eBooks are not doing as well as shorter things nowadays.

People don't want to read an eBook, or a 20 page item. They don't really wanna learn about something, they just want to fix an immediate problem, so, if you can do something more specific, so, the checklist and the blueprints are doing much better than the e-books and the more in-depth information nowadays.

Gene Clow:
How can you prevent that information from becoming somebody else's checklist, or somebody else's blueprint? Quite honestly, I'll send that when I'm in the throws of a listening or an acquisition. But I don't just put that information out there because my competitors would pick that up in a heart beat.

Paula Williams: That is a great point, Gene, and I think that is a concern that a lot of people have, they don't want to put things on their website. This is actually one step beyond that where people have to actually put in an email and a phone number, or give you some kind of information in exchange for that.

So, that's one way to take it one step away from being immediately plagiarized because you're taking if off your website and putting it behind some kind of a gate.

John Williams: But, But the other approach is to, particularly in your business, I know that you could probably say there are 12 to 15 very high level steps in acquisition or sales process.

Each one of those steps has probably got 20 to 30 plus steps in it. So you could give the high level version and nobody's going to know what's underneath it.

Paula Williams: Right.

Gene Clow: There's some truth to that.

Paula Williams: And also, just make sure that you got your, you distribute things as PDFs and you have got your contact information on every page.

Of course, that doesn't prevent someone from using it, but a trick, and I don't know if you've noticed with the, if Melania Trump's staffers had done this, they would have prevented a whole lot of problems [LAUGHTER] but whenever you purchase content from anyone and, you know, we do this with our writers, we do this with everyone.

When we get content from anyone, we will take a string of 12 to 15 words and just stick it in the Google search window. And see if something comes up. And the likelihood of that happening if it's original content is really low. Like trillions. So, you know, depending on how many words you pick and you know, it can't be something that is a direct quote.

But, we do that on a fairly regular basis with our content, because some of the other aviation marketing companies, and I won't mention any names, will rip off our stuff. And we show up on their website. And usually all it takes is just a quick email, saying, you know, we've noticed that you've published this on this date, we had published it two years prior.

Here's the page that we think it probably came from. You may not be aware that someone may have copied this, so we tried to be nice about it, but they're always very, very embarrassed, and they tend to not do that again for a couple of months until they hire somebody new who tries it again [LAUGH] .

John Williams: So, far we haven't had to take the next step, which is to have our attorney contact.

Paula Williams: Right.

John Williams: So, everybody seems to be straight forward and not going out of their way to do that.

Gene Clow: Yeah. I put that phone call over my company's name. And I didn't lose that one.

Paula Williams: There's also some software called CopyScape. That will do this for you. And just continuously runs to find out if there's anything published on the web that's the same as your material, so that's pretty cool. Catherine, I know you've produced a lot of this material.

Are you concerned about copyright. Is that something you've run into?

Kathryn Creedy: I haven't run into anybody violating my copyright, but I had a conversation at Oshkosh with some of the photographers. Who had their stuff blatantly stolen from their website. And I was shocked to hear that. When they did the nice thing and said, by the way this is a copyright.

You can buy it from me. It's X amount of dollars. They were blatantly told in no uncertain terms and expletive deleted you. And the photographers had to go after them with their lawyers, and they ended up paying no only their fine, but the lawyers' fees and the whole nine yards.

So it is something that's done a lot and done for not great purposes too. I mean, a lot of people had just want to rip things off and your experience hasn't been that and my experience hasn't been that, but it is something you have to be concerned about.

Paula Williams: Right I guess the good news and the bad news about aviation is that it's a small community so everybody knows everybody.

And if my philosophy is if you publish something and you have dates on it you know and you let somebody know after that that it's usually pretty embarrassing to them to be let know that and it's usually somebody like an intern or somebody in their office that they tasked with something.

So it's often inadvertent.

Kathryn Creedy: The big problem that the photographers and even some of the other writers were talking about, is that it's on the internet, so it's free!

Paula Williams: [LAUGH]
No it's not exactly. People work really hard on this stuff and work to produce it. So you do have to produce, I think it is worth risking putting content out there.

But you can keep it high level, you can keep it copyrighted, you can watch copy scape, you can test things and so on. So those are all ways to protect yourself once it's out there. And John, I know John and Rick, I think we have a new lead magnet for you that just started this week, so we I'd love your input on that as well.

If anyone has downloaded that and seen what that looks like, so.

Paula Williams: It's definite, yes.

John Williams: Yeah, I'm excited to get some responses from those and see where it goes. And like we talked about, you need challenges with an ultra small market as well.

Paula Williams: Right. Yeah, and Gene, to your point, if you make it super specific so that it's not really going to be useful to anybody except your ideal customer then the only people who would benefit from ripping it off is your direct competition.

Then you only have three or four people to watch.

Paula Williams: Cool. All right, next topic. Why do 98.6% of ads on Google get banned?

John Williams: These ads are adwords?

Paula Williams: Yeah.

John Williams: They're ad words?

Paula Williams: Correct. Pay-per-click adwords ads. And there's a lot of folks in aviation, especially flight schools that rely very heavily on pay-per-click ads. They spend hundreds of dollars a month on this.

John Williams: And in 48 hours, most of them are worthless and costing you money and quality on your website.

Paula Williams: Exactly, and the reason that they get banned is because of what they call irrelevance.

So where that the ad is about is, let's say in few type ratings and then the page that it goes to talks about flight training. So, Google, being a stupid machine, [LAUGH] or a very smart machine depending on how you look at it, can't tell the difference that this is actually related to that.

So, the irrelevance really has to be obvious if we're using Google ads as opposed to any other type of social media ads, they're a little bit more lenient about what those meanings are.

John Williams: And being Google, they won't even tell you this.

Paula Williams: Right. That's the crazy thing is you buy and ad and it gets banned and you don't even know that it's not serving.

So, you've paid for an ad, and there it is, not doing anything.

John Williams: And if it's bad enough, you can get dinged for it from Google, and actually lose ground instead of gain.

Paula Williams: I know. So your search engine optimization actually suffers. So, you know? Our suggestion is to have somebody.

We've got Boostability. You know somebody that concentrates on Google really. If you're going to be doing business with Google, they change things so often and it's getting so technical that it needs to be someone like that handling that for you. Anybody had any experience with Google Ads in the group today or

Paula Williams: Sounds like we'll move on. [LAUGH] So all right, quick sales tricks on LinkedIn. This is actually really cool, I like this a lot because a lot of the sales that we do is very specific. So LinkedIn really gives us a way to get to know people pretty quickly and to find the people that we want to work for.

Because we pick our clients very carefully, they all have to be people that we like, otherwise this doesn't work. And I know everyone on this call is really familiar with how that works. We really need to get to know folks to do that. And a lot of you guys are the same way.

The people that you do business with, Catherine, the people that you write for are usually people that you know very well, and that you have done a lot of research on and things like that.

Kathryn Creedy: That's absolutely correct.

Paula Williams: Yeah. [LAUGH]

Kathryn Creedy: And I do the research on LinkedIn.

Paula Williams: Do you? I know you post a lot on LinkedIn. You're probably one of the most prolific people that I know. So maybe you could talk a little bit about your technique and how it works for you.

Kathryn Creedy: Well, a long time ago, I decided to learn about social media.

I basically brought myself kicking and screaming into social media, cuz I thought, ugh, new task that I don't wanna learn, but if you're going to have any type of brand, it's absolutely essential.

Paula Williams: Mm-hm.

Kathryn Creedy: And one of things, and I've been collecting LinkedIn articles for awhile. And December and January are very slow months for me, so I decided one December that I would do nothing but LinkedIn when I wasn't working on articles.

Paula Williams: Yeah.

Kathryn Creedy: So I went through every single one of those articles that I had clipped on LinkedIn, and I adopted whatever it said if it related to me. And so I find LinkedIn is one of my most important platforms. And one of the reasons I do so much on LinkedIn is because with LinkedIn, you can establish an expertise very rapidly by posting to the groups that are salient to you and posted to LinkedIn in general and writing blogs and things like that.

So I actually get [COUGH] a lot of hits from that. [COUGH] Excuse me, and so the other thing about social media is it's not about creation, it's about curation, which also helps build your expertise. I wanna build my expertise with other aviation publications, so if I think they're gonna be interested in a subject, I'll go on Hootsuite, and I'll ping it out to Facebook, Twitter, and LinkedIn.

Paula Williams: Smart, very smart.

Kathryn Creedy: And I get a lot of retweets and I get a lot of comments on Twitter and not a lot of comments from LinkedIn, but that's okay. And people have, like you Paula, I have remarked that I do a lot on LinkedIn. And that's the whole point, to raise my visibility.

Paula Williams: Yeah. Right, that is absolutely right. And John you've got some experience on LinkedIn as well.

Jon Wenrich

CENTREXCONSTRUCTION, INC.
AVIATION • COMMERCIAL • INDUSTRIAL

- Centrex Construction
- CentrexConstruction.Net
- jon@CentrexConstruction.Net

Jon Wenrich: Yeah, ironically the single most beneficial or successful sales tool I've used for high network individuals, in particular in the last year, is the difference between clicking the Connect button that comes up from the network page where it shows pages and pages of potential connections.

If you click that, it sends the canned introduction message which I always ignore.

Paula Williams: Yeah.

Jon Wenrich: If you click the person's profile and then click Connect from there, it allows you to send the personalized message. And I always include my phone number in that, and I've gotten more calls immediately after sending that directly from a potential client than I have any other medium.

But it's the difference between that canned message and the personal message. And I would say I've done business with that person, as opposed to a friend or something like that, and nobody's ever questioned that.

Paula Williams: That is brilliant. That's what we found as well with high net worth and ultra high net worth individuals is often they will pick up the phone long before they'll hit reply.

And a lot of them are in John Williams demographic, and I know it drives you crazy when people are texting when they should just pick up the dang phone, right?

John Williams: Yes.

Paula Williams: [LAUGH]

John Williams: I mean, I get it, right. A text to say are you there, yeah, or a quick question.

But to get long-winded text, when you ought to be talking, just disgusting.

Paula Williams: [LAUGH] True, yeah and that just makes you a real person when you've had a conversation with them, as opposed to just an electronic exchange. So very smart to customize the message, very smart to include your phone number.

Paula Williams: Yeah, I think these are all really good suggestions from Kim, and they worked for us as well. So we always recommend people have a top ten most wanted customers and that you connect with them, you follow up with them. You send them, perhaps articles that you think would be relevant to them, congratulate them on their anniversaries and things and always change that canned message to you something else, even if it's a tiny change but make sure you do that.

John Williams: And another thing is, if you travel like we, most of us do, wouldn't hurt to have an updated picture because I've met people in restaurants when we both have not met each other before and decided to meet, so we looked each other up on LinkedIn, so we know who we're supposed to meet.

Paula Williams: [LAUGH] Doing the funky blind date thing, I'll wear a red carnation.

John Williams: You walk into a restaurant, and are you Joe? Are you Joe? Yeah. If you need the guy's picture, you just walk right up to him, so. It's crazy, but it works really well.

Paula Williams: Absolutely.

All right, okay, moving along. Which four social media does Kim think are unnecessary distractions? Google+, Twitter, Instagram/Pinterest, and YouTube. I use all four of those. [LAUGH]

Kathryn Creedy: Yeah, me too.

Paula Williams: Good, sorry, Kathryn.

Kathryn Creedy: All right, I do too, I don't use Google+, but I was just given a lesson at OshKosh that I should be doing Google+.

So I'll spend this December on it.

Paula Williams: Excellent. I do think that these are less vital than, most of our business comes from LinkedIn, Facebook second, if we were to categorize social media. [COUGH] Third, and then, we do get a lot of pressing queries and other things from Twitter.

So if you're after PR, Twitter is certainly a thing to do-

Kathryn Creedy: I thought that, when I've gone to conferences with the media, where it's a meet and greet specifically, PR to media. When you ask them what social platforms they use, they get their news from Twitter, Facebook, and LinkedIn.

So I've almost completely concentrated on those three platforms.

Paula Williams: Right, right. And Gene and John Williams I think you two pretty much exclusively use LinkedIn, is that correct?

Gene Clow: For what little bit of social marketing I do, that's correct.

John Williams: Yes.

Paula Williams: Yeah, great, and there's your demographic breakdown right there.

[LAUGH]

John Williams: But, not anything like them.

Paula Williams: Right. Jon, what about you?

Jon Wenrich: In terms of the ones I consume or submit too?

Paula Williams: Both actually. Let us know. Yeah, either both ways.

Jon Wenrich: For me personally, I've always been a little bit behind the curve relative to my millennial generation. So I rarely use Twitter, Instagram. However, my wife is heavily influenced by Instagram. I tell you what. [LAUGH]

Paula Williams: Yeah?

Jon Wenrich: All the time. But for producing, it's 90%LinkedIn. And consuming probably 80% LinkedIn.

Paula Williams: Okay, yeah, so you're right there with the guys. [LAUGH] That'll be another three on the call. One thing I have found which is kind of an anomaly in aviation is that they're in the pretty active Pinterest group for some of the vintage aircraft, and especially for aircraft maintenance.

It's surprising cuz you think Pinterest is housewives doing cupcakes or whatever, but actually there is a pretty active group that does modifications to an aircraft, and they take pictures of those. And then they have some groups on Pinterest and Instagram that are pretty active. For those purposes so it's an anomaly for the industry so that's interesting.

Kathryn Creedy: I bet you'd find the same with YouTube. YouTube is great for going to, to figure out how to do something.

Paula Williams: Yes, definitely. I think it's wonderful that you can figure out just about anything you want on YouTube. And a lot of the aviation maintenance folks.

And also aircraft aviation training folks do a lot on YouTube that's good stuff. All right, so the next section she talk's about is customer retention. And I think this is really interesting, because we're always focused on marketing new customers, new customers, new customers. But you can't use social media in a lot of cases to retain customers, introduce your customers to each other, build that network.

Help them use customer service and other kinds of things, using social media. So she talks about a 5% increase in customer retention can increase your profits, and she quotes the Harvard Business Review is 25 to 125% increase in profit. And from our experience, that is absolutely true or maybe even more than that.

Every customer retained is worth a lot more than a new customer that we acquire.

John Williams: And costs less to acquire, you're already there.

Paula Williams: Yeah, yeah absolutely. So and you guys, I know, often have repeat customers. Catherine, I know, people come to you again and again. I know we do, [LAUGH], come to you again and again because you're really good at what you do and we're comfortable with you.

So you probably write for the same people quite a bit.

Kathryn Creedy: I do, I have seven or eight different clients, but I write for the same ones every time. And yeah, somebody who'll be, that's good for diversity so that somebody won't be using me for a while. And somebody else will.

So it helps me even out the seasonality.

Paula Williams: Yeah.

Kathryn Creedy: But also, for instance, if I see an article of specific interest to one of my clients, I immediately put it up on their social media page. Or I immediately tweet it out or whatever and hashtag them or put their @ symbol there.

And I go out of my way to find their Twitter handle. And I always get it retweeted. And when I see them the next time or when I speak to them the next time they always mention how much they appreciate that little effort on my behalf. They don't pay me for that but I know that they're gonna be interested.

Paula Williams: Yeah and that they're gonna think of you the next time that they need something done, right?

Kathryn Creedy: Right.

Paula Williams: And Gene you're in an interesting business because people don't buy airplanes every week [LAUGH]

Gene Clow: In fact that was interesting because when I started out with you a few months ago the average was 32 months for aircraft ownership.

And I'm going to inquire with the multiple listing services to find out where that has changed. Because I honestly believe its moved way to the right.

Paula Williams: You think?

Kathryn Creedy: That's interesting because I was doing a story on financing at Oshkosh, and the two people I interviewed for that story, they both said the average lifespan of an aircraft for a particular owner was about five years.

So I hate to break-

John Williams: And that wouldn't surprise me in today's market for me, post 2004.

Paula Williams: Right.

Gene Clow: And John a quick question. What correlation do you find between the Amortization where we are moving up as well, and it's tied in hand and hand with the five year, what's the correlation there?

44

John Williams: I think it's a significant part of it. The fact that airplanes over the last four decades have been depreciating assets with a couple of exceptions. And very very short exceptions. Four, five year periods where people are actually making money on airplanes. But if you did the long term look, you're gonna see, prior to about the last four or five years, a constant 10% reduction on average per year.

The last four or five years it probably bumped up to 12 to 15%.

Paula Williams: Moving right along. I know there is probably a great conversation that the two of you could take offline with that. I think that because that ties right into both of your businesses as far as the length of time that people keep airplanes.

And how often they upgrade and or downgrade. But next question from the book. How important are beautiful pages emails, ads and other kinds of things?

Paula Williams: Opinions, thoughts?

John Williams: Well it depends on where you're sitting.

Paula Williams: [LAUGH] Exactly, this is that positioning that Gene mentioned.

John Williams: Well, we've had a client that wanted a quote, a beautiful ad and to say one thing but we tried to convince him it's a waste of money, would do no good.

He didn't believe it, so we put it out there and it did no good. He was throwing money away and subsequently, we couldn't convince him.

Paula Williams: Yeah. And there is nothing wrong with making an ad better looking as long as it does what it needs to do.

John Williams: Right.

Paula Williams: But I think the key here is really testing, and sometimes we find that ugly ads will outperform a beautiful ad. And beautiful is not necessarily the key to the kingdom here. What were after in marketing is a good return on investment. So, if we had a 5% on one ad and a 6% return on one that our client hates, [LAUGH], we're going to advise them to go with the higher return on investment.

John Williams: To be even more pointed, we acquired a client a number of years ago, before they got to us, had spent a quarter of a million dollars on their website. Boy, was it nice looking.

Paula Williams: It was beautiful. It was absolutely stunning.

John Williams: However, it's like buying a new airplane that's stunningly gorgeous, doesn't have any engines on it, because it was doing nothing for them.

They had not one sale in over a year's time from that website.

Paula Williams: Right. We had to mess it up a little to make it work. But it did work and that was the key point there. I think Kim makes it really, really well in the book. That's an excellent way to put it.

Paula Williams: What are the criteria for winning advertising awards? You may have wondered, winning the Clios or the Webbys or any of those other kinds of awards. People often think that that is an indication that you're working with a really fantastic firm, if they've won lots of Clios or lots of Webbys and things like that.

But actually, those are not indications that those ads are doing any better than any others. It just means that they were chosen by their peers and often that means that they buy a lot of advertising and have a lot of [LAUGH] brownie points with the industry. Would you agree, John?

John Williams: It's crazy because of the last statement there. Some of them didn't even have an ROI, much less a better one.

Paula Williams: Right. Exactly. The sad thing is sometimes the clever advertisements that win those awards, people will not remember what company they were from. They'll remember they really loved the ad and they react really positively to it but they don't know who it was from and it certainly doesn't directly relate to the product or service that's being advertised.

John Williams: You can test that yourself to Super Bowl time. Two weeks after the game, you can probably remember some ads but you don't what company it was and what product they were selling.

Paula Williams: Right, that is true. Next month, we're gonna be talking about Power Prospecting by Patrick Henry Hansen.

Check the events schedule for that. I want thank you guys for coming today. I'd love to have you guys tell us really quickly what you do and how people can contact you. Maybe we want to start with Gene?

Gene Clow: Certainly. Gene Claude with Great Circle Aircraft and I do the aircraft brokerage business.

We specialize in the lower 60s to the Gulfstream 650s and acquisitions and listings as well.

Paula Williams: Fantastic.

John Williams: Do you do Falcons as well?

Gene Clow: We do.

Paula Williams: John, may have some questions for you. [LAUGH]

John Williams: A little later on.

Paula Williams: Cool, Katherine!

Kathryn Creedy: I'm an aviation journalist and communication strategist, so I try to enhance the visibility of my customers into a subject matter expert and teach them how to do that whether by social media, I also write copy.

Paula and I have been working together. I write for about six or seven different publications on aviation. I'm one of the few reporters at the crossroads of business and commercial aviation and that's what I do.

Paula Williams: Fantastic.

Paula Williams: And Jon.

Jon Wenrich: Yeah, Ford and BMW can say they've built airplanes but would you trust them with your new corporate jet?

Paula Williams: [LAUGH] I might not.

John Williams: The same way many people say they've built the aviation facilities, hangars, MROs, FPOs but that's our fast ball, that's what we do and we're in it by choice. There's nobody better on the west coast than Aviation Construction because we know it and it's our passion so we're having a lot of fun. If anybody's seen the 12 acre Aviation FPO at PDX in Hillsboro, Aurora all over the West Coast. We're pleased to be in the industry.

Paula Williams: Beautiful. Thank you and we'll call it a wrap!

Which Digital Marketing Channel is Best for reaching Aviation Companies and Consumers?

Most Effective Digital Marketing Tactic for 2018

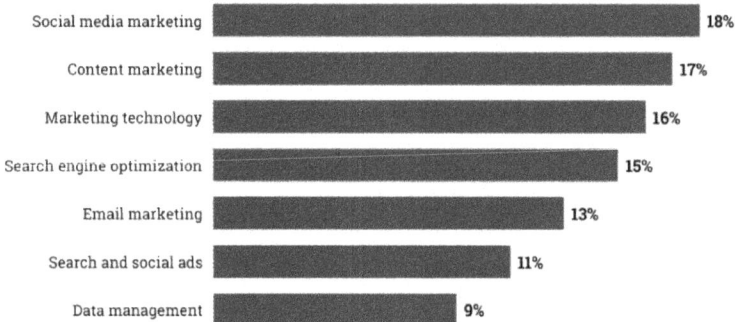

Tactic	Percentage
Social media marketing	18%
Content marketing	17%
Marketing technology	16%
Search engine optimization	15%
Email marketing	13%
Search and social ads	11%
Data management	9%

Published on MarketingCharts.com in December 2017 | Data Source: Ascend2 and its Research Partners

Based on a survey of 271 marketing influencers around the world from a mix of company sizes and primary marketing channels (B2B, B2C, B2B & B2C)
Figures show % indicating the most effective tactic used in a digital marketing plan in 2018.

Which social media channel is best for aviation professionals to reach decision makers?

We all have limited resources, especially time, these days.

And we're always hearing about newer, cooler, more interesting social media channels that may be better for our purposes.

In our experience, people vastly under or over-estimate the importance of social media for marketing.

Effectiveness Ratings for B2B Social Media Platforms

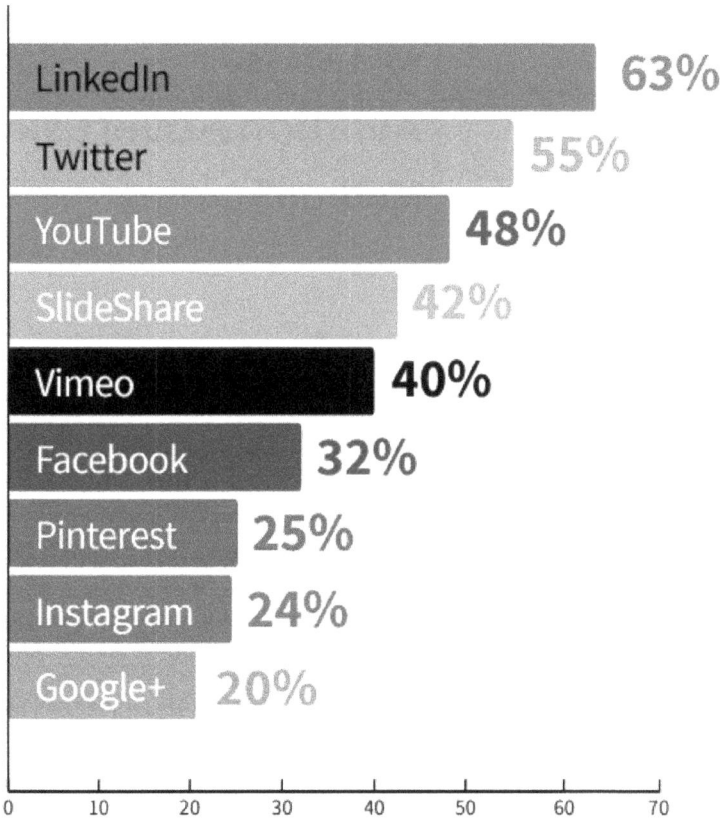

LinkedIn	63%
Twitter	55%
YouTube	48%
SlideShare	42%
Vimeo	40%
Facebook	32%
Pinterest	25%
Instagram	24%
Google+	20%

Source- B2B Social Media Strategy -SproutSocial.com

AMHF 0028 – What's the Best Aviation Advertising Media?

We're often asked -"What is the best aviation advertising media?"

Although the short answer is – "whatever works best for the least amount of time and money invested," the long answer depends on a number of factors, and the long answer is that this no one "best" advertising media, because none has all strengths and no weaknesses. The goal is usually to find the best COMBINATION of aviation advertising media that works best for your situation.

Many aviation sales and marketing professionals are frustrated with changes and shortcomings of different advertising media. They are looking for that one, perfect, trouble-free, cost effective advertising media that always works. The bad news? It doesn't exist. The good news? You can find a perfect combination of advertising media that does the best job for you.

Transcript – What's the Best Aviation Advertising Media?

Paula Williams: Welcome to episode number 28. Today we're going to be discussing, but probably not answering the question, what is the best advertising media for aviation, including international aviation advertising.

So I'm Paula Williams.

John Williams: I'm John Williams, and we're ABCI. ABCI's mission is:

Paula Williams: ABCI's mission is to help aviation companies sell more of their products and services. So before we get started, I want to give a shout out to Phil Rouin who suggested that we use a hashtag to market our podcasts and our webinars.

So, if you want to respond to anything that we say in our podcast or webinars or anything else, you can use the #avgeekmarketing, and we will reply to every tweet. And with respect to Chris Clark, who had a great article in the AirFacts Journal about why he hates the term "avgeek," we understand that.

[LAUGH] And also David Parker Brown from Airline Reporter who says "I am an avgeek, and hear me roar!"

John Williams: Well, I doubt we'll be roaring, but.

Paula Williams: That's true. No, there's always controversy about any issue that is important enough to discuss. And it's actually a pretty interesting conversation between the two of them.

If you want to look up both of those articles, you can Google them. Chris Clark's point is that avgeek kind of demeans the profession, and David Parker Brown says, dang it, who cares, so?

John Williams: [LAUGH]

Paula Williams: The profession does not need us to defend it. [LAUGH]

John Williams: No.

Paula Williams: Exactly, all right, so what inspired this particular episode is an article in the New York Times that was about how some of the media websites were having trouble with faltering ad revenue and traffic.

John pointed this out to me, and we had a conversation about it. Because if you are in marketing or in any industry, you're going to notice ups, downs, backwards and sideways all of the time. And it seems like it's getting more frequent and more disruptive as technology changes and as Google changes its algorithm, as ad people used different software to determine how much they want to pay for ads.

So the question is, is digital marketing really such a great thing? Is print marketing really such a great thing and so on? Another thing that happened this week is VDM came out with there advertiser survey which is actually a really good document. I hope you grab a copy of that, that included verbatim quotes from the people that responded to their survey.

And among the highlighted things that people said, print is dead. Or print is a break from the digital onslaught. Or print and digital are both important [LAUGH]. Editorial still beats advertising. And by editorial they mean of course, articles, cartoons, anything that is not, that doesn't look like a paid advertisement.

John Williams: Content is what-

Paula Williams: Content.

John Williams: The rest of us would call it.

Paula Williams: Exactly, digital has a low maturity level for the aviation industry. There were lots of really interesting comments from advertisers and from consumers of advertising in that survey that I think are definitely worth a read.

And if you are in this profession, you really need to understand what people are saying. And they did a great service by compiling all the information and making it available. That said, it is very contradictory and confusing. So what it really boils down to is, it's more than just a fight between team print versus team digital.

But it is much more complicated than just a fight between good and evil, or light and dark, or whatever it is that you see your side and the other guy's right?

John Williams: Well it shouldn't be regarded as them versus us. It's more logical this versus that.

Paula Williams: It is much more nuanced than that.

So today John and I played hooky in the middle of the day. And we got on the motorcycle, and we rode up the mountains a little ways from Tooele. It's just a little town in Utah where we live, and you can go up the side of the mountain.

Then you can look down on this whole little town, see things a lot differently than you do everyday. When you're in the middle of things, and you're looking at the gophers in the yard, and you're looking at the weeds behind the fence, and all of those other things, you kind of go nuts.

And what you really need to do when you're thinking about your marketing strategy and everything else, is not think about the tasks you have to do this week. But you need to really back up a long ways, look at your whole business, look at your goals for the year, and look at what's working for you and what's not working for you and why.

So rather than just simply the way most people phrase their questions to us are very, very detailed and having to do with a very specific situation or a very specific task. And a lot of times it is really, really helpful to just take a break in the middle of the day, drive your motorcycle up in the mountains.

[LAUGH] And look down on your business, as it were, as a metaphor. And just go okay, here's where we are, here's what's working. Here's what may not be, and see things from the perspective of a larger point of view, right?

John Williams: Absolutely.

Paula Williams: All right, okay, so the first rule of ABCI-

John Williams: [LAUGH]

Paula Williams: Our cardinal rule is "No random acts of marketing!" You really want to know what you're doing and why. This is really important when you are choosing advertising media, and there's a couple of other things to consider. One is that whenever you're advertising using some third party media or some third party tool or anything else, you are essentially playing football on someone else's field.

And this is actually a phrase that came up in an article by Cy Dawson, who was really, really frustrated because he had built an entire business on software that depended on Twitter which is one of the social media. And it was a great business, it had lots of software tools.

And it was really successful for a long time, but then they changed their terms of service and put him out of business. And in his parting comments, or his final article on his blog he said, you never want to play football on someone else's field. And there is a lot of logic to that.

But there is another side to the story, and that is that you will never get very good at football if you're only willing to play in your own yard, right?

John Williams: [LAUGH] Exactly.

Paula Williams: Okay, so it takes a variety of media to do great aviation advertising, some of which you control. And some of which are controlled by other people and entities who are going to change the rules on you.

And who are going to frustrate you and are going to raise prices on you, and going to do all kinds of crazy things that make you really frustrated and want to leave that media forever. But what you really need to do is consider the larger perspective.

John Williams: Well and sometimes you can't leave the media such as Google, they change everything every day.

Paula Williams: Exactly well and there's a lot of people who would love to leave google and just do things with paper only. And that is an option depending on your business but you certainly would pay a price for that.

John Williams: Yes.

Each medium has its pros & cons

	Trade Shows	Search Engine Optimization	Social Media	Direct Mail	Print Ads (Magazine)	Directory Ad
Results are measurable?	Possibly	Yes	Yes	Possibly	Possibly	Possibly
Targets people who are looking for what you do?	Maybe	Yes	Yes	Yes	Maybe	Yes
"Virally" spread from person to person?	No	No	Yes	No	No	No
Lasts until it's removed?	No	No	Yes	No	No	Stays 1 year
Targets people ready to make a buying decision?	No	Yes	Maybe	Yes	No	Yes
Results visible this week?	No	Maybe	Yes	Yes	No	No
Expense?	$$$	$	$	$$	$$$	$$
Effectiveness?	Very Effective	Moderately Effective	Moderately Effective	Very Effective	Moderately Effective	Mildly Effective

Paula Williams: All right, so let's talk about a few different advertising media and the pros and cons of each.

In no particular order we're going to start with websites so this would be like your own backyard right? You learn to play football in your own yard which is not a bad thing because you control everything about it, you can turn on the lights, you can only play when the weather is good, you can do all kinds of wonderful things that you can't do anywhere else because you control the format, you own the copyright to anything that you publish on the web as long as you put a copyright notice at the bottom of it.

You're protected in a lot of ways. There's a lot that you can do. You can control the colors, the fonts, the context, what's on the right hand nav, what's on your left hand menus, all of that stuff is within your control, assuming that you know how to do it, right? So it's a great place to really control your aviation advertising.

[LAUGH] Or you have a web master that is working with you or you're using a tool that is easy enough for you to manipulate yourself. So all of that is goodness. But the cons of that are that you have to keep up with a lot of technology, like for search engine optimization.

We recommend at least twice a year that you have a search engine optimization company look at your website, evaluate the key words that you're using, maybe do a SEO refresh to accommodate all of the changes that have happened to the search engines in the last. Weeks or months prior because they do changes things all the time on us don't they John?

John Williams: Yes they do.

Paula Williams: Right the other thing is you want to refresh the underlying technology of your website we recommend doing a refresh of your design every three years at a minimum because technology changes. And also the styles of the times, the fashion in website themes and look and feel of website changes.

There's new best practices and other kinds of things and you need to look like you're up on the technology and you're still in business. Aviation advertising is competitive, so you need to keep up.

John Williams: Is this because I can wear shirts I wore in high school doesn't mean I should wear them.

Paula Williams: Exactly.

John Williams: [LAUGH] Times have changed.

Paula Williams: Yeah, those things for men are not as different as things for women. Because men can still wear things that they wore a number of years ago. And they are vintage and cool and retro and all that other fun stuff.

John Williams: Mm-hm.

Paula Williams: Exactly. But you don't necessarily want your web site to look vintage and cool and retro right.

John Williams: Yeah not three or four years old it just looks like you've ignored it.

Paula Williams: Right and then the other thing is security. You do have to have security software and or people looking at your website on a daily basis if you're depending on it for your business.

Because things happen to websites no matter how well protected they are, hackers are sometimes one step ahead of you so you want to make sure that you have back ups and you're able to restore from a back up whenever you have a situation where something's been compromised or heaven forbid, hacked.

John Williams: And we're not going in too much details on this We had what we thought was good security. And then our Google Analytics said going down, and our Lexis going down and we said, wait a minute. So we ran a cross-report and discovered that some people are using our domain name and [LAUGH] putting pharmacy adds out there.

And it was very very interesting how they did it once we had somebody else figure it out. But now we have security people that take a look at our site every day, week, month, year, and it's relatively inexpensive but it's one of those things. I mean, if you don't know, you don't know.

Paula Williams: Right. So there is some constant upkeep, just like if you have [LAUGH] with a yard, with an airplane, with anything else If you own it you're responsible to keep it up. Otherwise it doesn't do you any good at all, because it becomes out of service, out of date, out of repair.

John Williams: Yeah, I mean I've been around long enough to… I built this site from scratch using notepad for God's sake. Tells you how long that was for a fortune hundred company. And now, of course, you wouldn't do that from tons of reasons, but even, I thought I was fairly up to speed on security and we figured out how they did what they did it was going to take us way too much time to fix it so we hired people to do it.

Paula Williams: Absolutely right so that's web sites that's kind of like playing football in your own yard. The good news is you're responsible for everything, the bad news is you're responsible for everything.

John Williams: [LAUGH].

Paula Williams: Okay. Trade shows are the most respected, most traditional media in aviation advertising. You can have in person handshakes and demonstrations.

You can do that anywhere else. So trade shows are a great place to meet a lot of people at the same time with only one air plane ticket right. So that's a wonderful thing but there is a problem with trade shows in that they are proliferating. It used to be that there were four or five major trade shows that Everybody went to, and if you went to those four or five pages every year, you would hit the major players.

You'd be able to meet with everyone in your market, basically cover all of your bases with the people that you wanted to meet with. In the last ten years though, the number of trade shows have proliferated to the point where there are hundreds of trade shows every year, just in the United States even.

If you look world wide there's probably thousands of trade shows on different topics and different specialties and different geographic areas and things like that. So they have proliferated a lot and also the cost of doing these trade shows has gone up quite a bit. Just in the years that we've been Appearing at trade shows.

Booth rent has gone up, they charge for everything. They charge for cleaning your carpets in between days. They charge for a garbage can.

John Williams: That's right, for the garbage can and to empty it.

Paula Williams: Exactly.

John Williams: At a "small" additional charge.

Paula Williams: [LAUGH] They charge for internet. There's ways around that.

You can bring your own sometimes.

John Williams: [LAUGH] They charge for electricity.

Paula Williams: They charge for electricity, anything that they can charge you for. It seems like every year the costs go up. Maybe 10%, or.

John Williams: And then they charge you for an extra chair.

Paula Williams: Exactly. It does take a bigger bite out of your budget than it used to, which is.

So, print ads, the next media we're going to talk about, in magazines and other kinds of things. So the pros are, they are also very respected, very traditional media. You can borrow the credibility of the magazine of you have placed an ad in aviation week then you can put an aviation week logo on your website and say this product is as seen in aviation week.

And there is a lot to be said for that especially for some newer products that don't have the name recognition, and you know that comes from an older brand and things like that. So It does it gives them psychological weight, gravitas, to maybe a new brand or a start up or something like that.

The cons of print ads in magazines are once again, proliferation. There used to be four or five magazines that everybody would read, and now there are hundreds of magazines. If you go to NBAA and look at the literature racks, you will see at least 30, I would say, magazines that you can just pick up a copy of every single one of them and if you are able to carry them home. And if you're talking international aviation advertising, that number goes up exponentially.

John Williams: And those are the ones, they selected to have in the convention, there are more.

Paula Williams: Right, so the number of magazines has really proliferated. Most of the individual magazines, I should say, have had declining readership in recent years where people are either going to a digital version or not taking that magazine at all because they are getting their information in other ways.

Readership is declining. Cost has not declined in proportion to that proliferation and that declining readership, so you're not getting as good of a deal for print ads as you used to. But it still is sometimes worth it for that borrowed creditability and that respect and being in that very traditional media.

John Williams: And as a number of magazines have proliferated, the amount of time people have to read them has gone down.

Paula Williams: Right. So they read them faster. [LAUGH] If they read them at all.

John Williams: Yeah. If they read them at all.

Paula Williams: Okay. Pay per click, getting into one of the digital media.

The pros of pay per click are that it is very, very fast. You can create a pay per click ad in 15 minutes if you know what you are doing and have it all over the Internet, internationally. There is no other way, that I know of, to make that happen that quickly.

It is also very effective for a particular keyword. If you do a really effective campaign and you've thought it out and you do it very carefully, that can get some really great response for a pay-per-click ad.

John Williams: That pre-supposes effectiveness is that you've chosen the correct key word or key phrase.

Paula Williams: That's why you need somebody who knows what they're doing, because you have to do the research to get everything right in order to make them effective. They are very nerdy, we don't recommend that the casual observer try and place a paper quick ad. It's gotten a lot more technical than it used to be, and there's a lot more people competing in that market.

John Williams: And it's more expensive and it's a good way to lose a lot of money and get nothing out of it.

Paula Williams: Right. So, since January, they have cut the number of pay per click spaces, at least, for Google ad-wares, which is the most popular paper click venue. They used to have Google ad words at the top of the search page, and on the side of the search page on the right hand side.

But they've gotten rid of those results on the right hand side. So they have half as many advertising spaces, and are charging the same amount for them, or actually charging more for them, because they have the same number of spaces. So you have to bid more to compete with the same number of spaces.

So the cons are that they can be very expensive for popular key words. And we only recommend them for things like empty legs or events or other things that you absolutely need to advertise right away and there's other way to meet your time objectives with other advertizing. All right.

LinkedIn a social media that is not considered a social media by those who hate social media, right? [LAUGH] You talk with a lot of aviation executives and they will tell you, I don't use social media or I don't believe in social media, but then you ask them do you have a LinkedIn profile, and they'll say, sure I have a LinkedIn profile.

That's different, somehow it ends up being in a different category than the other social media so the reputation of LinkedIn is better. So of the social media, I'd say it's probably the most respected, would you agree John?

John Williams: Yes, depending on what you're after.

Paula Williams: Yeah John is one of those that does not do social media but does have a LinkedIn account.

John Williams: Watch it now.

Paula Williams: [LAUGH] Right okay, so it's great for reaching professionals and business contacts but the cons are that their advertising tools are not as sophisticated as some of the other social media, particularly Facebook, which is probably the gold standard as far as their advertising options.

You know the ability to choose a campaign to reach a particular group of people that has particular behaviors and preferences and other known attributes that you really want to target. For international aviation advertising, this is pretty specific and helpful as well.

John Williams: You can really refine the demographics of what your looking for.

Paula Williams: Exactly, so LinkedIn is not quite that good, but it certainly is more respectable.

Facebook, if you look at the pros of Facebook numbers, this is the largest audience that you can get even of the aviation demographic. Especially for general aviation and some of the recreational aviation. It can be very effective, they have very low cost advertising options, and very granular campaign options.

Where you can target specific behaviors, characteristics, and re-targeting of people who like a particular page, or like a particular company. Or have a particular behavior. Maybe they have purchased a home in the last year, or purchased a car in the last year. You can find that out on Facebook, and you can't anywhere else.

So it's just scary, the number of things that you can't target, very specifically using Facebook.

John Williams: That's going to be like big data, right?

Paula Williams: Big data.

John Williams: [LAUGH]

Paula Williams: Yeah, and you don't have to be a big company. This is one of the ways that are very small company can take advantage of big data because they collect it, they manage it, they give you a nice little dashboard, by which you can do this.

It is kind of nerdy. So it is something that I wouldn't recommend doing a large campaign yourself until you either get some training, or get someone to do this for you.

John Williams: And watch them do it the first time.

Paula Williams: Exactly. So, the cons of Facebook is that it's not seen as credible by some in the aviation industry.

There are a few, I'd say maybe half, of the decision makers in aviation who are older, they tend to be 40 plus, they tend to be male, they tend to be former military, they tend to have security concerns and other kinds of things. About half of that group, and I'm going to call them the aviation decision maker demographic, feel a little weird about Facebook.

John Williams: They won't admit they use it, even though they do.

Paula Williams: [LAUGH] Right, but lot of those people have been dragged into Facebook, kicking and screaming by their grandchildren. And started to use it as users. And so lot of those folks, and that's why I'm saying half. So half would not touch it, half have been dragging, kicking and screaming into that world.

All right.

John Williams: But nonetheless, that means they're there so when you do re-targeting, they're going to see it.

Paula Williams: Exactly. True, that's as users, not necessarily as advertisers. Yeah. Okay, so video and YouTube. So when we are talking about videos on YouTube, we're talking about two things. One could be live video, where you stick a camera in front of somebody and take video, the other thing could be slides with background music or voiceover made into a video file.

Right? Either of those two things fits into the category that we're calling video or YouTube. Fair?

John Williams: Sure.

Paula Williams: Okay, great. So this category is great for product demos, facility tours, explanation of complex concepts, introducing employees, especially your sales people or customer service folks where you want to profile somebody and make it look like, make people feel more familiar with the particular person.

So that they feel more comfortable picking up the phone and talking to that person. It's a very effective way to make a connection with a perspective customer. These are often also shared between people so somebody at a company sees something they like, they will pass it to a colleague or coworker or boss.

And say have a look at this and tell me what you think. So, it's more likely to be virally spread than a lot of other media. The con's of video or YouTube are that it is labor intensive or cost intensive, if you're hiring someone else to do it to produce good video.

John Williams: Well define good. If you mean broadcast video, which you don't need, yes it's extremely expensive.

Paula Williams: Right. But even YouTube quality video, you do need to shoot it, you need to edit, you need to put it together, you need to upload it, you need to put the key words on it.

All of those things.

John Williams: But you're talking 1,000s versus 100,000s different.

Paula Williams: Yeah. Absolutely. You can produce a fairly decent video that is effective, that is not necessarily studio quality and polished for 100s, or 1,000s of dollars as opposed to 100,000s of dollars.

John Williams: Right.

Paula Williams: That video used to cost, right.

Okay moving right along, webinars and podcasts. One of the really great things about this we were actually just talking with a client yesterday about this. If you have a competitor that copies everything you do, this is a great antidote for that, because if you do a webinar or a podcast it is an incredibly difficult act for your competitor to follow.

Even if they did the same topics and everything else they are not you, so they can't replicate the same personality and the same style that you have. And if you're occupying that space first, they are very unlikely to follow you Into that space.

John Williams: [LAUGH]

Paula Williams: They'd be crazy to follow us in here, right?

John Williams: That's right.

Paula Williams: And that's the cons, it is labor or cost intensive to do a regular webinar series or a podcast. So either you have to hire somebody to do that for you or you have to do it yourself. And it is pretty labor cost intensive to do a good one.

John Williams: We were dragged kicking and screaming into creating [LAUGH] an audio video studio so that we could do all this stuff.

Paula Williams: Exactly, this is not where we expected to be, but it is so effective that now we're recommending it. All right. So every medium has it's pro's and con's and the moral of this story really is that there is no one medium and everybody is always asking us, they tell us I'm really frustrated with this particular medium, I don't want to do it anymore, I want to do something else, what should I do so I don't have these problems?

And the answer is everything has its problems, everything has its pros and cons. So.

John Williams: It depends on your target market.

Paula Williams: Exactly, so what we really need to do is sit down and have a look at your objectives and what media you're using now, and then cover the weaknesses And multiply the strengths of what you're doing now.

So if you look at a chart that shows the pros and cons, and there's one that you can see in the show notes for this session. And we just picked a couple of things like trade shows, search engine optimization, social media in general, direct mail, print ads, directory ads. In the U.S., and for international aviation advertising. What are the pros and cons of each?

And you'll notice if you look down those columns, there is none that is perfect. The ones that are really good at one thing will not be so good at another attribute. So you really want to cover your bases and you also want to make sure that you are playing football on your own field and you're also playing football on other people's fields.

If somebody changes the rules on you so that you can't play on a particular field no problem, you've got plenty of other places to play all right.

John Williams: And if you're in a car you're not going to see this anyway.

Paula Williams: [LAUGH] Exactly. Right. So the other thing is you want to, when you create materials, advertising materials, articles, videos, content whatever advertising materials you create, you want to think about being able to deploy them in more that one format.

So as an example, we do this podcast, we have a transcript of this podcast created, we post it on our website. We post little chunks of it on social media. We publish it on iTunes as a podcast. We use bits and pieces in some of our webinars and things like that.

Some of this is going to end up in our printed newsletter, which gets sent to people in the mail on paper made from trees using varial technology. So when you think about creating material you want to create things that are versatile enough that you can turn it into multiple forms of advertising without a whole lot of work.

John Williams: Instead of starting it on Twitter and have them change things you started it on your website.

Paula Williams: Hm-mm.

John Williams: You've diversified and split it out where if they change things on one social media you don't care because you're everywhere else anyway.

Paula Williams: Absolutely, so if Twitter goes away tomorrow or Instagram disappears or LinkedIn changes its rules or your favorite magazine raises its prices so that it's out of reach, or your favorite trade show has a hurricane and doesn't have a show that year, there's lot of things that can happen.

And if you have multiple venues of advertising, diversity really equals stability, right? And when we did our prospecting webinar, we used the example of a little kid fishing for the first time is going to dip a line in the water, and be just absolutely thrilled if he caches a fish.

But he has one line, and he caches one fish at a time, which is great. But if you are in business, you really can't depend on that one line. You really want to have multiple lines. And we use the example of a trolling boat. That has multiple line in the water at any given time and is using multiple kinds of bait, multiple lengths of lines, other types of things so that they are diversifying their angle of attack here [LAUGH] and making a different approach to all of the different fishes.

Some of the them are going to like one things better than another and you have a much better chance of having a stable business if you're not dependent of any one line producing a fish. So, download our tip sheet, the tip sheet this week is our design brief template.

We offered that to people that came to our free branding webinar. But this is a really great way to think about using your materials in more than one way. So your webinar should be branded, your podcast should be branded, your Twitter, tweets should be branded. Your Facebook posts and so on.

All of those should be branded in a way that makes it clearly identifiable as your material and that's a really good way to diversify across those things. So.

John Williams: A good quote to end on. Go sell more stuff, America needs the business. Guess who said that. I gave you five seconds.

You're probably wrong, but Zig Zeggler.

Paula Williams: [LAUGH] Exactly, I think we have that away, last week, but that's okay. If you didn't get it, or if you forgot, that is a really good quote to remember. In fact, you should print that out and stick it on your wall, if you're in business.

John Williams: And, the reason that works is because the multiplier effect in a capitalist market.

Paula Williams: Absolutely, every dollar you make is more than a dollar added to the economy which is a wonderful thing. All right so subscribe to our podcast, subscribe on iTunes, Stitcher or now on Google Play and leave us a review.

John Williams: And we'll see you next

Transcript – Print Vs. Digital, Round 2!

fter last week's episode, we received lots of comments from people advocating . . . (drumroll, please) PRINT media for aviation advertising. We decided to dedicate an entire episode to encouraging the use of at least one print element in every marketing campaign. The trick is to use print in a way that makes the most of its advantages (credibility and convenience) while mitigating its limitations (untraceability and cost) by integrating print and digital elements in a powerful campaign.

Reports of Demise of the Mailbox were Premature

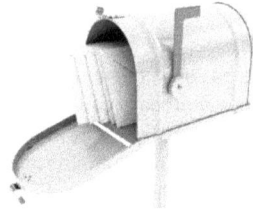

Paula Williams: Welcome to Aviation Hanger Flying, Episode number 29. Today we're going to talk about Digital versus Print, Part 2. I'm Paula Williams.

John Williams: And I'm John Williams, together we are ABCI. And our mission is-

Paula Williams: To help aviation companies sell more of their products and services. So just recently we started using a hashtag for conversation about our podcasts or our webinars or anything else, for that matter.

We promise to reply to any hashtag that uses, or any Tweet or Facebook share, or anything else that uses this hashtag and we will reply to every Tweet. So that hashtag is #AvGeekMarketing. All right. So now our motto is "No random acts of marketing!" We want to know what you're doing and why.

So after last week's episode, when we talked about print versus digital and some of the pros and cons of each, some people, of course, everybody has an opinion, don't they, John?

John Williams: Yes, they're like other things. Everybody's got at least one.

Paula Williams: All right, and some people have more than one.

John Williams: [LAUGH] Yeah.

Paula Williams: Which is fine, too, but a lot of people are very, very biased in favor of digital right now because it gives you the opportunity to see who's clicking on your links. You can do some great analytics. You can account for your money a lot more effectively than you can in print.

Another thing that it allows you to do is spend less money and also you can work from anywhere. So if you don't have a physical location, it's kind of hard to do print unless you outsource that to a great print shop like we do, right?

John Williams: Exactly.

Paula Williams: Okay, but there's a great quote from Mark Twain, that the rumors of my death have been greatly exaggerated.

And we found that the same is really true of print, reports of the demise of the mailbox were premature. There was probably an equal or greater number of emails and tweets and other things that we got indicating that they really like the aviation catalogs. They really like the printed publications.

They really like a lot of those things. And John, I think you fall into that camp, is that right?

John Williams: By and large, I like pieces of paper. I prefer books that are on paper in front of me that I can flip back and forth. Yeah, you can't put a bookmark like you can on some of the readers, but that's okay.

You also don't get the opportunity, in my opinion, to flip back and forth and reread stuff just because you can recognize what page it came from.

Paula Williams: Exactly, and John really is, we like to say, our target demographic in the aviation industry. Gender, age, military experience, education, all of that stuff usually falls squarely within the category of this is the perfect person to market to.

So the things that John likes tend to be the kinds of things that work really with aviation customers, so we take that very seriously. One of the problems with the aviation industry is that, especially when you get really specific, a lot of our companies sell very specific products that are components or software or maintenance processes, services and things like that for a very specific group of people.

And it's really hard to do testing for a very specific group of people. And it's hard to have statistics on hand about what's going to work for them and what's not going to work for them, so we like to use statistics from some bigger companies. And one thing that we got in the mail from a friend of ours that's in one of our Mastermind groups, and of course it came the week after we did our last podcast, was a really great article, Direct Mail Breaks Outdated Marketing Assumptions.

And this is by Sean Buck, who's in one of our Mastermind groups. And we'll tell you a little bit more about him in just a minute. But if you are familiar with Costco, and who's not familiar with Costco, right?

John Williams: Exactly, they're everywhere, they're everywhere.

Paula Williams: They're everywhere.

And they're one of those companies that has the numbers that is able to do the kind of testing that we wish we were able to do,

Paula Williams: In the aviation industry, right? [LAUGH] Yeah, our studio's got everything but an espresso maker.

John Williams: [LAUGH] You still can't make up for the fact that sometimes you need a drink of something to get your throat clear.

Paula Williams: Exactly, so, Costco sends 8.6 million magazines and catalogs per month. They are the third largest monthly publication in the world. The average member who receives a Costco Connection has a household income of 156,000 which actually puts them in the affluent category. And 56% of their members who receive monthly magazine buy something based off of what they read in the magazine.

John Williams: That's crazy.

Paula Williams: That's crazy. Now it's really hard to isolate, and especially with print, it's very, very difficult to say, did they see it in the store first and then see it in the catalog, and then they mentioned the catalog when they called in to buy it.

We really don't know, and that's-

John Williams: Unless.

Paula Williams: Yeah?

John Williams: Unless there happens to be a, what do they call those little things, those QR codes?

Paula Williams: QR codes.

John Williams: Something you can zap with your smartphone and if you do it right, then when they zap that, you know where it came from.

Paula Williams: Right, but there is a limitation with that. It only shows the last action before they took that action. So you don't know if they were in the store the week before, and came in and looked at the thing and sat on the patio furniture that they're going to buy, and did all of the crazy things that they want to do during the research for this product before they actually made the purchase.

John Williams: Yeah, but does it matter?

Paula Williams: It does, it does matter. But the point being, we have to go with the numbers that we have. We have to go with the best information we can put together. So you could say that what if they didn't do print, okay, so, they did a test.

And actually, during the Great Recession, which was 2008, 2009?

John Williams: Seven, I think, or-

Paula Williams: Yeah, somewhere-

John Williams: Between 2007 and 2009, somewhere in there.

Paula Williams: In that category, whenever they actually say that that started, they,

Paula Williams: Considered discontinuing the print version of their magazine. And they did a survey, and found that their affluent members, which is pretty much all Costco members, overwhelmingly prefer the print edition.

Ginnie Roeglin, the Senior VP of Costco's e-commerce and publishing, says she expects the print edition to the magazine to continue to grow in circulation for many years to come. So when a company as big as Costco is making decisions like this, then companies as small as some of the ones that are in our membership, or our group of folks that do marketing for aviation products, really should sit up and take notice because they have numbers that we will never have.

And they can do testing that we can never do, and they can do research that just makes us drool. Okay, you might say, well, Costco is just odd, and maybe it is. These are people who buy cases and cases of toilet paper, right?

John Williams: And sell the same like that.

Paula Williams: Exactly. But Williams-Sonoma is actually the parent company to seven companies, including the Pottery Barn and West Elm. But 50% of their company's marketing budget is spent on printed catalogs each year. And that's for the seven brands including Williams-Sonoma, Pottery Barn and West Elm. So once again, we have an affluent clientele.

We have the opportunity to do digital. If you've ever been to Williams-Sonoma's website, you know they've spent a lot of money on that thing. I mean it's got some beautiful photography, it's got recipes. You could spend days on there on their website. But they spend at least 50% of their budget on print.

Now if we could get away without doing print, we would. We would much prefer to be able to work from anywhere. We would much prefer not to have to turn our conference room into a mailing room every Friday to send out catalogs and other kinds of things. But we found that these things are just much more effective than we would like them to be for those of us who prefer print or for those of us who prefer digital because of the trackability of it.

All right, so you could say, and maybe you will, hey, Costco and Williams-Sonoma and those brands are older people. And you do have a point there, but here's another brand, and this is Bonobos, which is actually kind of one of the younger, hipper men's clothing brands, I would say.

And [COUGH] you would think that a younger hipper men's clothing brand would concentrate most of their money and time and energy on the web, right?

John Williams: Yes.

Paula Williams: Well, 20% of Bonobos' first time customers are placing orders because they received a printed catalog in the mail.

John Williams: Crazy.

Paula Williams: Yeah, so it is crazy, but the same catalog buyers are spending 1.5 times as much as first time buyers who did not receive a catalog and who were just buying online. So there is still a tradition in this country, and as far as I know, this is all US, if anybody's got data from elsewhere, I'd love to see it.

But still, people are doing a lot more purchasing based on paper. And I'm not sure if that's the credibility factor, if that's the convenience factor of having something in your hands, what exactly is it that's causing people to spend money when they have something on paper rather than online?

And I think if you had to boil it down it would probably come down to credibility, wouldn't you think?

John Williams: I'm not sure because we at, what's that magazine I can't pronounce, Hanneker and-

Paula Williams: Hammacher Schlemmer, yeah.

John Williams: [LAUGH] And I like to look in it because you can look at pictures and it just seems more, maybe it is credibility, seems more real.

You see a picture, you see it described. And yeah, you can do all that on the web but somehow it's different.

Paula Williams: Yeah, well on the web you can see the pictures move, they have videos and things.

John Williams: Yeah, I know, but with rare exceptions, you can bypass the video because you can let your brain work on that, right?

Paula Williams: Mm-hm.

John Williams: And you see, but you read all of the pertinent data and, I don't know, it just seems, I can sit on a couch with a cup of coffee and peruse that. I don't have to be at my desk. I don't have to be worrying about what to do with the mouse and spilling coffee on the keyboard.

So, I don't know, I'm not quite sure really, but to put too fine a point on it is I wouldn't know what to say, but I like the magazine.

Paula Williams: Okay, and I would say that Americans for generations have been trained to look in catalogs, figure out what they want, whip out their credit card and make purchases ever since the old JCPenney catalogs.

John Williams: Which makes you wonder and gives you pause, If Amazon were to put a catalog out.

Paula Williams: How they would do, and that's a good question. It'd be interesting to see. And what would they put in it? I mean, they've got such a huge inventory.

John Williams: Well, it'd be like the old Sears catalogs from way back when you went to a catalog store just to look at the catalog.

Because the catalog's so huge, you can't lift it. That's right, talk about a four-inch thing with microthin paper

Paula Williams: Mm-hm, okay, so one more example. Neiman Marcus has found that they get $4 back in sales for every dollar that they spend on producing, printing, and mailing a catalog.

Now that is absolutely staggering. Now if you could make $4 back for every dollar that you spend on a particular kind of advertising, you'd just be shoveling every dollar you could get your hands on into that form of advertising.

John Williams: Absolutely.

Paula Williams: And you'd do that all day long.

John Williams: That's crazy.

Paula Williams: It is, all right, so obviously, print still has a lot of validity and anybody who is thinking about completely eliminating print from their repertoire is out of their mind so-

John Williams: And should think again.

Paula Williams: And should think again. And you know this is interesting because with every client we have ever had, we always end up having to arm wrestle with them to get them to do anything with print, and it's partly because of the expense.

And I understand that.

John Williams: True.

Paula Williams: And partly because of the inconvenience, because you end up getting some return address, or return bad addresses and other kinds of things.

John Williams: I think probably the negative isn't the client. They've all put glossy ads in magazines, a one time shot for one month out of 12.

Or maybe even recurring and they got no way to track, and they don't think it does any good.

Paula Williams: Because they did a random act of marketing.

John Williams: That's right.

Paula Williams: It didn't work. They think print is bad.

John Williams: Or maybe it did work and they don't know how to prove it.

Paula Williams: Yeah, so it was not replicatable because it was not part of a system. So whatever you do, you need to make sure that it's disciplined, and it's measured, and it's part of a marketing system. But, every marketing system should include some print. And I can't think of any scenario in which there would be an exception to that.

But yeah, I told you about Sean Buck. He's a great guy. He's in a lot of our Mastermind groups. And he runs a company called The Newsletter Pro. And what they do is they put together newsletters for different companies. And he specializes, I think, in dentists and a lot of other professions, service professions, things like that.

And we may end up doing some business with him in the future for our clients, so stay tuned. We'll keep you informed as we like to leverage smart people's brains in different specialties that are outside of aviation course. So, and you could make the argument, what does all this have to do with aviation?

Okay, all the examples that we gave you were affluent customers, right?

John Williams: Yes.

Paula Williams: Mm-hm, some of them have older customers and most of our aviation clients also have people who are in their 40s, 50s and above, things like that as their target customer. Some of our folks, like the software folks and the training companies, are targeting younger male customers.

So that would be similar to Bonobos and their target market.

John Williams: And some of the young folks, they call them nouveau rich? [LAUGH]

Paula Williams: Yeah, exactly, the software kids, the Silicon Valley folks.

John Williams: Well, whatever, I mean they're 30, give or take, and have money to spend.

Paula Williams: Absolutely.

But in all of these examples, their numbers are larger than ours. There is no way that we would be able to test an 8.6 million piece mailing. Costco can do that. Nobody that we know could.

John Williams: Even our marketing group, when they do split testing, they do it on several hundred thousand, rather than millions.

Paula Williams: Exactly, so when somebody has a really big set of data that, and John, you can talk more about how much more reliable statistics are when you have a larger sample set, right?

John Williams: Of course, the larger the universe, the more you can test, the more the numbers mean something.

Paula Williams: Exactly so that's a problem we're constantly running into in aviation is the small test size can be thrown off by one or two outliers that really mess up our numbers, right?

John Williams: Yeah, and if you threw out the outliers, what you have left is not much because of the size of the universe.

Paula Williams: Exactly, right, okay, so what does this boil down to? What does this mean to you? We think that you should include at least one print component in every campaign and we do this all the time. We try to include at least one print component, and here's some examples on how you can do that.

You can have a postcard that leads to a call to action on the web. For example, go to this web page and order a free book about this topic. Or you could send a printed catalog that goes to online demos and videos of each of your products. That's one way to combine print and online.

Another way you can combine print and online is you use online leads. You use online lead capture like some of the very highly targeted, re-targeting or Facebook ads and other kinds of things to get people to your website to request a printed information package. In all of those examples, you're using online to save money and to track your numbers and to do all of the wonderful things that print does for you while you are also including one print element that gives you that credibility and that advantage that print does, right?

John Williams: Yep, and you should listen to your customer. If they say they want more printed matter, then consider that.

Paula Williams: Exactly, so a lot of folks that have a newsletter or whatever, you could always ask your customers if they want the printed version, the online version or both.

Because if they want both, it doesn't cost you any more to also send them the online version. And you really, really, really do need to have a printed newsletter, I think, that you send out at least probably quarterly, depending on your customers, and depending on what you're doing, so.

All right so, the freebie this week is still our Aviation Brand Design Brief Template.

Paula Williams: The template is actually a really good way to show some consistency so that people can see when they get one of your printed materials and then they go online having those design elements, your logo, your colors, your fonts.

All of those design elements will really help you maintain a consistent appearance, whether you're using print or whether you're using digital. And that's something that we've seen a lot of errors and a lot of problems with in aviation is where they have one department doing their print, or they outsource their print maybe to a print shop or a graphic designer that specializes in print.

And then they have their webmaster do all of their online graphics, and then they end up looking like two completely different companies. So you don't really know for sure. At least there is a moment of uncertainty when you take that printed catalog and then you go to buy something online and it looks like a completely different company.

John Williams: Consistency is key here.

Paula Williams: Mm-hm.

John Williams: And you may not have to go as completely nutso on consistency as some of the big names like IBM and Wells do, but the more consistent the better.

Paula Williams: Exactly, and using that brand template will help you do that across the board regardless of whether you're using subcontractors or printers or other folks to do some of that work for you.

All right, so go sell more stuff. America needs the business.

John Williams: Zig Ziglar.

Paula Williams: Yep, absolutely, subscribe to our podcast, Aviation Marketing Hangar Flying. It is on iTunes, Stitcher, and Google Play. And please do leave us a review. See you next week.

John Williams: Ciao.

Old Rules, New Rules, & Reality in Aviation Marketing

In David Meerman Scott's book **The New Rules of PR and Marketing**, he explains the differences between the Old Rules of Marketing and the New Rules of Marketing.

The Old Rules of Marketing

- Marketing simply meant advertising (and branding)

- Marketing needed to appeal to the masses.

- Advertising relied on interrupting people to get them to pay attention to a message.

- Advertising was one-way: company-to-consumer.

- Advertising was exclusively about selling products.

- Advertising was based on campaigns that had a limited life.

- Creativity was deemed the most important component of advertising.

- It was more important for the ad agency to win advertising awards than for the client to win new customers.

- Advertising and PR were separate disciplines run by different people with separate goals strategies and measurement criteria.

None of this is true anymore. The Web has transformed the rules and you must transform your marketing to make the most of the Web-enabled marketplace of ideas.

While we agree with Meerman-Scott that the web has transformed marketing, we know that a great advertisement is still a powerful part of a campaign. ABCI also subscribes to the theory that aviation companies don't typically have the mass market appeal, nor the resources invested of a Coke or Pepsi. Traditional brand advertising is not the best use of funds or the most successful way to reach aviation decision makers.

Over the past few years of working in the aviation industry, we've confirmed our suspicion that a significant number of decision makers are male, mature, many have a military background, and do not fit the typical "silicon valley" profile of an internet or social media user. But most do use the internet (or have their staff do it) for things they want to buy.

Regardless of whether they're reading a magazine ad or a web page, they respond to clear, concise, convincing writing.   They need good, solid information to support their decisions.

Aviation is a unique niche. It requires intelligent positioning and targeting. It requires respect for the industry and the professionals within it.

Fighter Pilots, Marketing Execs, and OODA

How fast is your OODA cycle?

It's a question of critical importance to fighter pilots, who are taught to act quickly to:

Observe

Orient

Decide and

Act

(In the midst of a dogfight.)

It's also very important to marketing and sales professionals. We may not have people shooting at us or have our lives hanging in the balance on the typical Monday afternoon. More often than we probably believe, we are facing a decision that holds the livelihoods and fortunes of our coworkers and families in the balance.

Unfortunately, the results of our decisions are also not as clear. This may cause us not to recognize an error until months or years after the fact, if ever. We all know of sales and marketing execs who were "asleep at the switch" and allowed an opportunity to pass by, or permitted a competitor to acquire a key client simply because they failed to **O**bserve, **O**rient, **D**ecide and **A**ct in time.

Here's what we mean, in terms of sales and marketing:

Observe:

- Do you have an editorial calendar of industry publications and trade shows? (ABCI CONSULTING CLIENTS DO!) Do you know what will be discussed when among your peers?

- Do you read industry magazines? If so, do you notice who's advertising more or less than last month?

- Do you attend industry events? If so, do you notice whom among your competitors, clients, and desired clients are there? How much money did they apparently spend on their booth, on after-hours parties, and on giveaways and contests?

- Do you watch Google Analytics or WebTrends for your company's website? Are you getting more or less traffic this month than last? How are your competitors doing? (ABCI WATCHES THIS DATA DAILY, AND REVIEWS IT WITH EACH OF OUR CONSULTING CLIENTS MONTHLY.)

- Do you have frank and open discussions with your current and prospective clients about what is changing for them? How will the price of gas affect them if it goes higher? Are they concerned about coming changes in regulation or the economy? Are they worried about tax changes or the "fiscal cliff?"

Orient:

- What conclusions can you draw from what you've observed? Will you be the first or last to know of a change in the market?

- Do you have the ability to modify your product or service offering to take advantage of a new or emerging trend?

- Do you brainstorm opportunities and risks with a mastermind group or informal group of key stakeholders and clients?

- Do you regularly set aside time to think through your "Plan A, Plan B and Plan C?"

- Does your company have (or can you create) the capacity to generate multiple streams of income, or is your company a "one trick pony?" What can you do to diversify?

Decide:

- How many people are involved in the decision-making process? How long does it usually take to make a change to a product or service, or a marketing campaign?

- Are you comfortable making decisions based on incomplete information? (Most decisions are made this way – if we waited for ALL of the relevant data, the opportunity will have passed us by!)

Act:

- Do you have a complete marketing system that is flexible enough to change a component and get quick, accurate data on how well it performs?

- Do you have segmented marketing lists, a receptive and responsive Twitter and Facebook following that helps you spread the word about a new product or campaign?

- Are you able to change your website quickly to accommodate a new campaign? (Can you add a new landing page, response form, and content within a day or two, – AS ABCI CONSULTING CLIENTS CAN – or will it take longer?)

- Do you have long- or short- term advertising contracts? If they are long-term, can you change the content at will?

Sales and marketing are not easy in the current economy. Ten years ago, you could run the same campaign for years and expect to have reliable results. In this competitive environment and changing economy, it requires a lot more hard work and resources to keep (or expand) your market position. It also takes a quick and effective OODA cycle!

This cycle can also be used to evaluate social media –

- Observe what's going on with social media channels – are your customers and competitors using (or talking about) something new?

- Orient by researching the pros and cons of each social media tool, and its suitability for your current marketing tasks and priorities.

- Decide, usually as a 90 day test. Use a social media channel as part of a campaign.

- Act! Add the channel as a "permanent" part of your marketing system. Note that even traditional media aren't really permanent – magazines have fluctuating readership, trade shows have fluctuating exhibitor and attendance numbers, and postage rules change.

Marketing Analysis – In God We Trust, All Others Must Bring Data.

"How nice it must be to have such a creative job," people say when I tell them I'm a marketing consultant.

I always have to smile to myself.

For every creative task, there are about five tasks that involve crunching, analyzing, generating, percolating or figuring out how to capture data.

Data makes the difference between a powerful, reliable marketing system and "random acts of marketing."

Many (otherwise sophisticated and intelligent) companies throw time and money into one marketing attempt after another. They may buy an ad in an aviation magazine one month, participate in a trade show the next, and begin a Facebook campaign the following month, without relating these disjointed tasks to one another, or even relating them to a goal or objectives any more defined than "we need to make more sales."

A complete and powerful system integrates each marketing and sales task into a complete system where each part complements the others.

Each component of this marketing system can be measured.

Using that data, you know whether to invest more, the same, or less (or skip altogether) any of these related steps next time. When you have a solid, working system and you only change one thing at a time, you know exactly how much difference it makes when you switch out one component at a time.

Even if, like many businesses, things are moving too quickly to be scientific and disciplined, keeping excellent records will give you early warning if something makes a big difference, either positive or negative. When that happens, you can easily test your hypothesis and isolate the factor that made the difference. And capitalize on what works, and minimize what goes badly.

Even if you don't change anything, the markets are changing around you. Keeping track of your marketing data lets you know when something changes – maybe you have a competitor you didn't know about, or a seasonal spike in demand that you weren't aware of. Data tells you where to spend your time and resources- both of which we could all use more of!

Here are numbers that should be tracked:

- Length of your "sales cycle."
  How much time elapses between your first contact with a prospective client and when that prospective client makes a purchase?

- Expenditure and return on each of your marketing channels
  How much are you spending, divided by the number of dollars generated by sales attributed to that item?

- Number of leads, (you may also call these prospects or contacts, depending on which books you've been reading lately)

- Number of leads that each next step in your marketing and sales processes

- Rate of "closure" (How many of your leads eventually become customers?)

There is always a surprise or two lurking in the data. Even clients that are VERY sure that they know their market very well, and "know what works and what doesn't" find out that their staid, conservative prospective clients are using Facebook in huge numbers, or that they respond better to an inexpensive postcard than a beautifully printed catalog.

Some of these numbers take awhile to get a handle on, depending on the length of your sales cycle. In many aviation-related businesses, the sales cycle may be months.

Tracking them isn't difficult; it's simply a matter of keeping scrupulous records over time. Whether you keep you records in a spreadsheet or in CRM software (customer relationship management software like InfusionSoft or SalesForce) your data is a gold mine for improving your sales results over time.

Social Media in Long Cycle Marketing

Why Long Cycle Marketing?

Random Acts of Marketing are seldom profitable, particularly in the aviation industry, and particularly in a less-than ideal economy.

The aviation industry has some key differences from marketing to a more general audience.

- **Trust is more important.** Large-ticket, high-value or complex transactions have a higher risk associated with purchase decisions.

- **More information is required.** Aviation professionals like to know a lot more than "regular people" do about products & services they purchase.

- **Sales cycles are longer.** More people tend to be involved in the purchase decision, which adds time to the sales process.

Our specialty is **Long Cycle Marketing**. This style of marketing is particularly effective in the aviation industry; as well as other large-ticket, high-trust or complex products and services. **Long Cycle Marketing** is characterized by a systematic approach that includes an incentive for targeted prospective clients to "opt in" based on an informational incentive (usually a free white paper, report or ebook.)

In exchange for high-quality information the prospect then begins a cycle of progressive, long-term, low-key, low-cost and educational contacts using a mixture of media, including social media, direct mail, email and other methods as determined based on the demographics of the target prospect. **Long Cycle Marketing** is designed to position our client as the knowledgeable expert and source of information on the topic, as opposed to being viewed as a salesperson or vendor. The prospect is thus moved further along the sales process. After the sale takes place, **Long Cycle Marketing** continues to nurture the relationship so that testimonials, referrals and resells become a natural consequence.

Of course, this whole process depends on publishing *interesting, high-quality, relevant content* that your customers enjoy reading or viewing. We produce excellent articles, podcasts, and video to educate your customers and prospective customers about the unique value you bring to the table.

How Does Social Media Fit Into Long Cycle Marketing?

There are several points where social media can accomplish specific tasks.

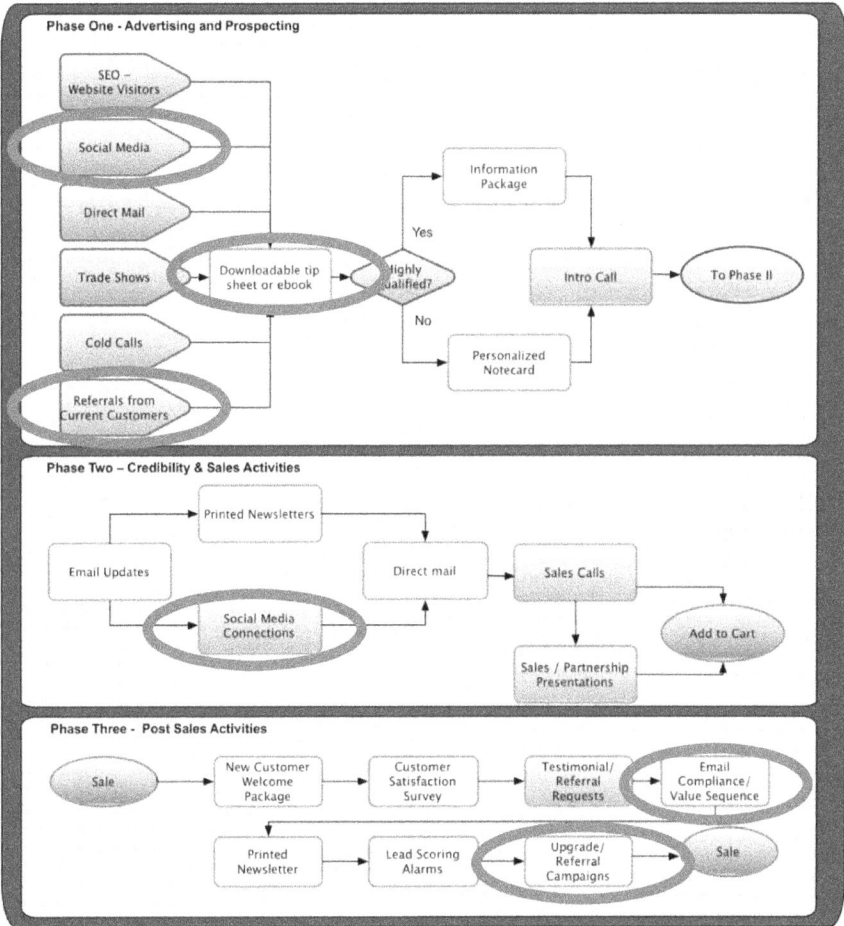

Social media is simply a tool. Tasks in a marketing system that can be accomplished efficiently include these:

Phase One – Advertising and Prospecting

- Acquiring new leads (in this example, we use social media to offer a downloadable tip sheet or ebook.)

- Acquiring referrals from an existing client or fan.

Phase Two – Building Credibility & Closing Sales

- Maintaining contact with a prospect during the pre-sale period.

- Providing "information snacks" to educate the prospect about the product or service

Phase Three – Post-Sales Activities

- Providing information like customer service or a "tip of the week" to encourage use of the product.

- Requesting referrals and resales.

As with any rapidly-changing technology, many clients over or underestimate the importance of social media.

The same principles that apply to any other communication medium (such as the telephone) apply to social media. It can be an invaluable tool, or it can be a complete waste of time.

Social media channels are proliferating and there are conflicting reports about the effectiveness of any particular channel for marketing.

Here is our litmus test to determine if you should use a particular social media channel:

- Are your top ten most desired future customers using it?

- Are your top ten most competing activities and clubs using it?

- Are your top ten most important partners using it?

If the answer to all three questions (or a majority) is yes then we should consider that social media channel as a communication tool.

Using Social Media In Campaigns

Why Bother Planning Advertising Campaigns?

Many of our new clients (or people who aren't clients yet) ask us:

"What's wrong with just running an ad and seeing how it does? Why bother planning advertising campaigns? I have enough to do!"

I understand where you're coming from – none of us needs extra things to do to keep us busy!

General Dwight D. Eisenhower, who knew a thing or two about planning, and about being busy, said this:

Plans are useless, but planning is everything!
– Gen. Dwight D. Eisenhower

Obviously, the simplest thing to do is something we call a "**random act of marketing**." An ad salesman from a magazine, trade show, directory, group discount program, web site or email "blast" company calls and asks something like:

"Wouldn't you like to get your ad in front of 10,000 people who are looking for just what you offer? We're running a special this month and you can get a hundred dollars off if you sign right now."

This sounds good, so you sign up.

Then one of two things happens:

You get lots of calls and visits from "looky lous" and "freebie seekers" who take what incentive(s) you're offering and move on like a cloud of locusts.

Absolutely nothing. The phone doesn't ring any more this month than it did last month.

What went wrong?

A failure to plan! A "**random act of marketing**" is almost always a waste of time and money!

"Saving time" by jumping into an ad contract without planning an effective campaign is a false economy.

"Saving money" by having someone who is inexperienced or unqualified on your staff plan your campaigns is also false economy. (Even if it's you! I know better than to do graphic arts. Our graphic artist knows better than to plan her own marketing campaigns.)

A great campaign consists of a list, an offer, and the presentation.

- **The list** is ideally some reasonable number of people who are "prequalified" in some way – you have reason to believe they need what you offer.

- **The offer** is a specific transaction that you are proposing. "Get your airplane serviced here, and we'll detail the interior free."

- **The presentation** or media has to do with how the offer is presented to the list. This could be in a phone call, a visit, an ad, an email, or a trade show booth.

Both of the problems can be prevented by planning these three elements well – we look at each circumstance case by case, but can only determine a cause if the campaign is well-designed to begin with. We need data to diagnose!

1. "Looky Lous" and "freebie seekers" are often the result of too general a list, or too generous an offer.

2. No response at all to an ad could happen if you're using the wrong media to reach this audience, or the offer is not attractive enough to your target audience.

Campaigns should make the best possible use of the list of prospects by presenting them with a series of thoughtful, relevant ads in different media, all of which contribute to an overall impression of your company as a trusted provider of the product or service they need.

- Each step should have realistic expectations of what should happen.

- Each step should have measurable criteria so that you can clearly determine whether or not "it's working."

- Each step should have decision points to evaluate what to do next based on the results

Few (if any) campaigns go precisely according to plan, but like General Eisenhower, we simply can't afford to be out there without a plan!

And in case you don't believe Eisenhower, here's another one -

"He who fails to plan is planning to fail." – Winston Churchill

Action Items

Trying to get by without a plan almost always results in wasteful "Random Acts of Marketing." If it's worth spending time and money on, it's worth planning!

Three Reasons Aviation Companies Should Run Marketing Campaigns

"Why should aviation companies run marketing campaigns? Why can't we just find a price that works, create an ad that works, and keep running that all the time?"

This was the most intelligent question we've had in a long time – unfortunately the person who asked it wanted to remain anonymous!

It stands to reason – objectives of any great company that cares about its products and its customers wants to do the following:

- Create a great product, always.

- Provide something of value, always.

- Charge a fair price for that product, always.

The Three Elements of Successful Campaigns

- The List
- The Offer
- The Presentation

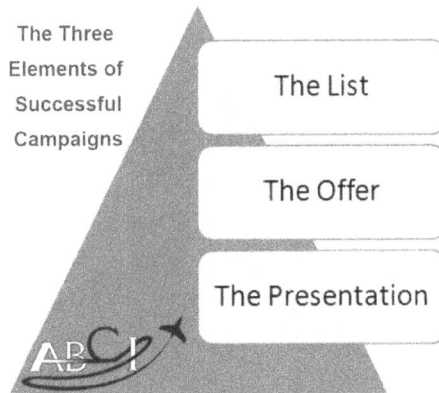

These are worthy objectives, and to many business people, seasonal or temporary campaigns can seem like unnecessary disruption of normal business practices at best, and shady underhanded dealing at worst.

We agree! We've all seen the people on street corners waving signs screaming "50% OFF! THIS WEEK ONLY!" week in and week out. We've all bought products only to find out that they went on sale the following week and we feel like we overpaid.

Disingenuous campaigns can ruin your credibility and your relationships with regular customers.

Having said all that, why do we still recommend campaigns?

Here are three main reasons campaigns can be absolutely vital to meeting your sales goals:

Engage With a Sense of Urgency.

If you've found that prospects are progressing through your sales process and agreed they need your product but never quite committing to the sale, you may need to find a reason to convey a sense of urgency. If your prospects are telling you "I love your product and I'm going to buy it someday," you can't exactly make payroll and pay your bills based on those promises. You need to communicate some reason that its in THEIR best interest, as well as yours, to make the purchase a priority!

We advise reasons that convey reality. If your product can be connected with a seasonal issue or a regulatory change, take advantage of the natural deadline to encourage customers to buy. If you offer a service that helps your clients come into compliance with a FAA or TSA regulation that is going into effect on a certain date or time, it's a natural opportunity.

You can also communicate internal reasons as well – provide customers an "inside view" of some of your internal dynamics and let them take advantage of your naturally slower cycles can be a win-win opportunity. We offered a discount to clients who engaged us several months before our busy season before NBAA. Clients that engaged us for NBAA-related services in August were charged a lower rate than those who engaged us in October. Why? Because when we have to hire additional people and/or pay overtime, it's reasonable that our prices reflect those charges.

To Experiment With a New Product or Package.

We all have to adapt to changes in regulations, technology, and competition.

If you have a software product for pilots, there is no doubt that you've noticed the increase in the number of pilots that carry iPads and tablet computers.

When you develop new version of your product, (perhaps to be compatible with new devices, for example) there are several campaign techniques you can use:

- Offer discounts to early adopters and "beta testers."

- Offer your older versions at a discount

- Offer free upgrades if one is nearing completion

If you offer something else, like charter service, you may wish to "try out" a bundled service like ground transportation or hotel discounts before you engage in a long-term marketing relationship with a potential partner. Offering a short-term "deal" gives you the opportunity to see if your customers are excited about it, if your partner lives up to his promises, and if all goes well before jumping in with both feet.

You may want to try out different "bundles" of your own services to increase transaction size and encourage loyalty. If you offer aircraft maintenance, for example, you may offer a loyalty program that offers discounts or additional services like a detail cleaning with a phase inspection.

To Bring Back Old Customers

We've often said that the "money is in Phase Three" in aviation marketing, (Phase Three being repeat sales and referrals.)

We advise clients to run a special campaign once or twice a year that focuses attention on your existing or past customers, this is a great way to ensure you're capitalizing on your greatest asset – the people who already know, like and trust your company. Referral campaigns can be a time to specifically reach out to your existing customers and ask for referrals, or "friends and family" events can offer something special to your past and existing customers and entice them to refer friends or family for a special discount or bonus.

There is probably a natural cycle to repeat purchases – one of our clients knows that his clients tend to make a purchase every three years. He keeps in touch with them during that three-year cycle with continuous newsletters and birthday cards, and at about the thirty-month mark he makes a note to give them a call and find out how business is going and how things have changed. Those calls bring in new business.

Action Items

Wondering where to invest time and money in your marketing system?

Phase Three investments almost always have the best ROI.

How do you measure the effectiveness of your marketing?

"What gets measured gets improved."
— Robin S. Sharma

Most businesspeople, especially those involved in aviation, are very disciplined about how they handle production management, service implementation, legal and regulatory requirements management, and last (but not least!) financial management.

They are not as disciplined about their marketing.

This is a mistake. Finding new customers and managing your relationships with them is one of the most important functions of your company.

Number Ten in Jay Conrad Levinson's Sixteen Monumental Secrets of Guerrilla Marketing is this: "Use **measurement** to judge the effectiveness of your weapons."

The fact that business owners don't manage marketing as rigorously is usually not because of negligence, but because many business people are not clear about what they should be measuring; how to go about collecting the information you need, and how to make decisions based on the information you've collected.

Ask the right questions

Asking the right questions (deciding what factors are important enough to measure) is the most important part of this process. If the questions aren't meaningful factors in your sales process, then all the data collected, reports written, dashboards designed and decisions made are pointless, so it's important to be clear on your sales process. Once you are clear on the steps, you can ask meaningful questions. For example, if your marketing campaign is centered on a trade show, consider the following questions:

- How many current contacts did you invite to visit your booth (for a free gift or demo, for example?)

- How many of those current contacts responded to your invitation?

- How many new contacts were made at the show?

- How many of those contacts were followed up with?

- How many sales were made subsequent to a contact at the show?

Collect data

Collecting data to answer your questions can be done with various technological means. For example, you could send invitations to your trade show booth using an email program that tracks opens and responses, or you could have used Facebook and tracked the number of "Yes" responses.

For mailed invitations, you'll simply have to count and respond by hand, unless you have a mail service that will do that for you.

At your booth, you may use badge readers or a goldfish bowl in which you collect business cards and later check them off against a list.

Marketing data collection is often time-consuming and involves some work. Technology is great, but since marketing includes personal interaction, the persons doing the interacting have to be aware of what's being counted and the expectations and processes for reporting on their interactions.

Reports, dashboards and views

We like Google Analytics because it gives us great data in an easy format without any work on our part.

So, we can determine where traffic to our website is coming from, which articles are getting the most views, and even how much time people are spending on our site. It's a great example of a dashboard.

Unfortunately, most of our sales processes involve a mix of online, in person, by mail, by email, and on the phone contacts. The only way to really see the whole picture of a sales lifecycle is to document all of these methods in a contact management database. We (ABCI) use InfusionSoft. There are others like SalesForce or ACT that are also excellent. But any system is only as good as the data that gets entered into it. So if your salespeople and customer service folks aren't documenting every phone call or interaction, you're not seeing the whole picture.

Whatever you use, make sure that it's set up properly, that your people are trained to use it, and that it's part of an incentive program. Easy, automated systems that are tied to real money get used. Difficult ones fall into disrepair and reports become meaningless.

Action Items

If you've invested in CRM software, you're wasting your money if you don't also invest the time to learn to use it well! Make it a practice to spend time weekly learning something new.
(We use Webinar Wednesdays for things like this!)

Make decisions

Once you have a great report that shows the typical sales process, refine it. Do more of what works and less of what doesn't. You may find that an expensive ad is having no effect. Don't continue to run it simply because you always have. You could invest that money in a part of the process that has a more measurable outcome.

We review data with our full-service clients once a month; and make major decisions once a year. Since the sales cycle in aviation takes so long, it often requires a year to determine whether a channel (like a trade show) had any impact.

And each year, we review everything; starting with: "Are we asking the right questions?"

Getting Things Done

The Digital Citizen – Why You Should Hire One (Or Be One!)

Cartoon- www.joyoftech.com

Some people always seem to know the best way to accomplish something using the Internet. They know how to set up an event in Facebook. They're the ones you call in a panic when you're in a video teleconference and things go haywire. They are up on the latest news about your industry because of things called Google Alerts and RSS Feeds. They can get the CEO's latest keynote address published on YouTube. And they do all of these things faster and more easily than any of their colleagues. Brian Halligan and Dharmesh Shah have a term for these folks, coined in their book *Inbound Marketing*. They call these people "Digital Citizens."

Salespeople used to be hired based on their communication skills (as we determined from interviews and phone calls) and on the size of their Rolodex- how many decision makers in the industry they had access to.

Now, it's equally important to hire based on **modern** communication skills (which includes video teleconferencing, tweeting, and a dozen other things we didn't care about five years ago) and the size of their following and influence on the Web.

The four factors that Halligan and Shah include in their list of New Hire Requirements for everyone (leadership positions, sales, marketing, and even customer service) are some degree of each of these qualities:

Digital Citizens
Google your prospective new hire. Digital Citizens usually have an up-to-date profile in two or more media (LinkedIn, Facebook, Twitter, Del.ici.ous, Google Plus) and include some industry-related articles, videos or posts in each.

Analytical Chops
Ask your prospective new hire to bring his favorite spreadsheet and explain some counter-intuitive insight that came from analysis of data. This type of person may have bumper sticker on his car that says "In God we Trust, all Others Bring Data."

Web Reach
People that are influential on the web with your prospective customer demographics bring much more than their personal skills to the job. They bring new credibility and reach. Benet Wilson recently changed jobs from Aviation Week to join AOPA's team recently – we think AOPA got a huge bargain, because Wilson had a huge (in aviation industry terms) following on the web. She had 909 Facebook friends, her Twitter account @AvQueenBenet had 14,000+ followers, and her blog www.AviationQueen.com was a favorite with aviation news junkies. AOPA's marketing now gets to benefit from the people that take Wilson's expertise into account when making a decision or purchase.

Content Creators
Some people can write an effective article about your product or service and post it to a LinkedIn group. Others can easily create a screen-captured demonstration of your software and post it to YouTube. Still others may capture a trade show event with a digital camera and post it on your company blog. Each of these people is creating a valuable, lasting asset for your company's marketing efforts. Whether these persons are actually in the marketing department, or whether it's the guy that does your taxes and shoots video as a hobby – this is a skill that should be sought out and rewarded.

Calculating, Rewarding and Encouraging Digital Citizenship

You can estimate the "digital citizenship" of your company by evaluating the reach of your leadership, sales, marketing and customer service personnel. Assuming that each of the following people publishes industry-specific information or does active networking in the industry at least occasionally, here's an example:

	LinkedIn Followers	Twitter Followers	Facebook Friends	Blog Subscribers
Jane, CEO	134	0	10	0
Joe, CMO	65	0	35	0
Marvin, PR	500+	293	453	15
Linda, Marketing	500+	695	298	200
Totals	1199	988	796	215

Total "Digital Citizenship Score" for the company – 3198

Our example company is doing well for a small firm- having a total "Digital Citizenship" score of more than 1000 means that you have the potential to use new media in your marketing. Companies like Zappos and Amazon (or NBAA or Cutter Aviation, to use aviation examples) probably have numbers in the millions.

Hiring people who are Digital Citizens, or encouraging your current staff to cultivate the traits listed above, is a great way to position your company to communicate as consumers increasingly expect.

Action Items

It's never too late to become a "Digital Citizen." And it's always to your advantage to control your image online.

AMHF 0013 – 6 Prospecting Methods Using Aviation Digital Marketing

Aviation Digital Marketing has lots of appeal these days, and for good reason- it's quick, it's inexpensive, and it's very easy to measure results. It offers the "instant gratification" of running a campaign and getting results in less than a week.

If you think of your marketing campaign as a campfire, prospecting via digital marketing is like kindling – it gets things started quickly so that you can move on to the more substantial parts of your sales process!

The six methods of digital marketing we talk about in this podcast are:

1. Search Engine Optimization

2. Content

3. Videos

4. Podcasts

5. Webinars

6. Social Media

So, let's get down to it!

Transcript for Prospecting Methods Using Aviation Digital Marketing

Narrator: You're listening to Aviation Marketing Hangar Flying. The community for the best sales and marketing professionals in the aviation industry. You can't learn to fly just from a book.

You learn from other pilots who know the tools, the skills and the territory. Your hosts, John and Paula Williams are your sales and marketing test pilots. They take the risks for you and share strategies, relevant examples, hacks, and how tos. Be sure to subscribe to iTunes so you won't miss a thing.

Paula Williams: Welcome to Aviation Marketing Hangar Flying Episode 13, online prospecting using aviation digital marketing tools. I'm Paula Williams.

John Williams: And I'm John Williams.

Paula Williams: And we are ABCI.

John Williams: ABCI's mission is to help you folks sell more stuff and products and services and quickly in the aviation world.

Paula Williams: Exactly. So we get our information from a lot of different places.

And with online materials especially it is really really hard to stay up on the changes in technology and everything else. So we go to a whole bunch of different conferences and mastermind groups and everything else each year to talk with people in other marketing, who are in marketing but in other industries besides aviation, because a lot of folks are using different tools with different results, that haven't really tried them in aviation before.

And so you know a lot of these are tried and true, a lot of these things were trying for the first time. And that's why we're doing this episode is to let you know, what the top six are as far as the online prospecting tools for 2016, so that you're getting the most current information.

Okay. So the top six prospecting tools for 2016 as far as online tools go are these:

John Williams: SEO.

Paula Williams: Or.

John Williams: Search engine optimization. And you have content and videos, podcasts, webinars, and social media.

Paula Williams: Exactly.

John Williams: Not necessarily in that order.

Paula Williams: Right, okay, so those are the six and we're going to talk some more about each of those six methods of digital marketing, and how you can use them for prospecting and how people get clients in the aviation industry by using these tools.

So starting with search engine optimization, which is probably the most cost effective. Wouldn't you agree?

John Williams: Typically, depending upon if you get taken by somebody who doesn't know what they're doing, but if you have your own staff does it or if you hire a reasonable, knowledgeable.

Paula Williams: Reputable.

John Williams: Firm, then yes.

Paula Williams: Right exactly. And there are a lot of shysters shall we say or snake oil salesman, in the field of search engine optimization. And the reason is because it is so technical that most people just kind of wash their hands of it. We used to have an SEO "Do It Yourself" kit that people could buy.

It was an information product that people could buy and basically do search engine optimization on their own. And this was in 2009 when search engine optimization was easy enough for a human to understand who actually had other jobs in the world, and that wasn't the only thing that they did besides eat and sleep.

But things have changed since then.

John Williams: Technology is changing almost daily with respect to what it is that Google and the other heavies want with respect to how you place words, phrases, content, and meta data and so forth. And I mean changes daily several times but the major changes are the ones we try to keep up with and we hire people to do search engine optimization for aviation companies.

Paula Williams: Right, absolutely, so we're kind of getting ahead of ourselves. Let's go back and talk a little bit more about advertising and prospecting in general and then we'll get more into the details of each of these items. So, phase one, as we know in our long cycle marketing process, is advertising and prospecting, which is the way that people first come into contact with you, or with your company, or with your product.

So, they're looking for something, you happen to be in the right place at the right time to catch their attention and engage with them in a way that really starts a relationship. And in the last episode we talked a lot about calls to action. So each of these items you're going to have to have a really great call to action.

It doesn't really matter if you have a really good ad. Unless you get somebody's attention, and get them to take the next step towards you. Either by calling a phone number, or downloading a report. Any one of a number of things. And in the last episode, we had a freebie that you could download that had 17 ideas for what we call lead magnets, or calls to action for these kinds of things.

So that's kinda the big picture. And of course, today, we're drilling down to the online methods of advertising and prospecting. Now a couple of episodes ago, we also talked about the concept of getting your prospects to identify themselves. And we told the story of Perry Marshal's friend the professional gambler.

Do you remember that story?

John Williams: Keep going.

Paula Williams: Okay, so they walked into a casino in Las Vegas, and the first thing he told this kid that he was trying to teach gambling to was, the first thing you need to know is, who is a prospective gambling partner and who is not.

And the way that they did that is, he pulled this sawed off shotgun from under his coat, and he cocked his shotgun, or racked the shotgun I guess is the terminology they use.

John Williams: Pulled the slide back, ejected the shell, or even if no shell, you just pull the slide back and snapped it forward.

Paula Williams: Right, now, this makes not very loud noise if you're talking about a loud casino with music and dancing girls and everything else. But it does get the attention of certain individuals in the room who are familiar with that sound. So what our gambler said to his young friend is, these are the people you don't want to gamble with.

These are the kind of people who know what a shot gun sounds like. Those are not the kind of people you ever want to have anything to do with, as far as gambling goes, especially gambling for fun and profit, right?

John Williams: Yeah. Because they're the charlatans, etc., and card cheats and so forth.

Paula Williams: [LAUGH] Right. Okay, so what does this story have to do with the price of rice in China?

John Williams: It's your story, keep talking.

Paula Williams: [LAUGH] Okay, the reason we're telling this story is because you have to do the same thing. You don't need to necessarily rack the shotgun to sort people into one pile or another.

Either people who are interested in your product or service, or people who are not. But you do need to do something. That is going to be a very distinctive signal to people who are obviously in the market for your product and service. And that could be by offering a buyer's guide to a particular product.

It could be by using language and wording that only airline maintenance people are familiar with, or that only pilots of a Kingair 350ER are familiar with. That's the way you separate The wheat from the chaff. Or you separate the prospects from the people who are not likely to be in the market for your product or service, right?

John Williams: Exactly.

Paula Williams: Okay, cool. All right, and every aviation marketing campaign has three elements, right?

John Williams: And you all should know them so you can say them along with me.

Paula Williams: [LAUGH]

John Williams: The list, the offer and the presentation.

Paula Williams: Exactly, the list, the offer and the presentation. So, every time you do an advertisement, the list is the people that the advertisement is going to appear to.

The offer is what are you offering. In [LAUGH] similar words, what is the thing that you want them to do. And then the presentation is the form that that takes. Is it a webpage? Is it a brochure, is it a form, is it an email, is it a social media.

John Williams: Or a telephone call.

Paula Williams: Image yeah exactly so those are lists, offers, and presentations. So choosing online marketing tools. You want to think about the list, who is the list of people who are most likely to buy your product. And where do they already hang out online?

John Williams: Which means you have to know the demographics of your potential customer list.

Paula Williams: Exactly. And a lot of people will argue well, my customers don't hang out on Facebook because I don't hang out on Facebook. Therefore my customers don't possibly hang out on Facebook, right?

John Williams: They may think that but you can't assume anything, because everybody knows what assume means.

Paula Williams: Right. You want to think about where does your list hang out online. What do they do when they're online? What kinds of things would they be looking for? What kinds of words or phrases what they be typing into Google when they're looking for your product or service.

Where can you get in their way when they're looking for the product of service that you offer? And also what gives you the best venue for your presentation. So, if you got a great video or something like that you want to take them to your website. Right?

John Williams: Or to put it another way, wherever all the cars are driving you want a billboard on that road.

Paula Williams: Exactly. You don't want to build it on a beautiful fabulous LED monster billboard on a dirt road with one car a day. Right.

John Williams: Right.

Paula Williams: Okay, so we've talked about prospecting, sorting people into, these people are interested in my product or service and these people are not.

So how do we apply that to search engine optimization or SEO? Okay, what we do is we start with a spreadsheet. We use Google Analytics and it's actually a free tool that you can use. We do this for all of our clients. So if this is getting too nerdy, you can always just give us a call [LAUGH] and we can handle it for you.

But if you want to do it yourself, basically what you do is you go to Google Analytics, there's a free tool called their keyword planner. And in that keyword planner you want to brainstorm all of the words and phrases that your customers are likely to use. So, you just type them in.

You can type in a list. You can add a website and have it spider that website for you, meaning that it will go through that website and look for all of those keywords. And you can do that with your own site, you can do that with your competitors' sites which is really cool [LAUGH] but anyway, you come up with a list of several hundred key words.

John Williams: Sometimes several thousand.

Paula Williams: Sometimes several thousand key words and what we do is we like to sort them by three things. The most important being relevance and relevance is not something you're going to get from Google's keyword planner because they don't know what you sell and they don't know how relevant these keywords are to you.

You have to remember this is a robot, so it does what it does and it's not very intelligent. So there is place where human human connections and human thought processes are not duplicatable by any kind of a machine. So you have to determine which of these phrases are relevant to you once you get this big list.

John Williams: In other words, what that means is you've got to go down through every single keyword or keyword phrase. And assign a relevance factor of one to three.

Paula Williams: Exactly. So then you take all your one's and that's your first sort criteria. Your second sort criteria is how many global monthly searches are there on that keyword?

Now the more the better. Again we want lots of traffic. On this road that we're going to place our billboard on. So the more global monthly searches the better. The next factor we want to look for is competition. How much competition is there? And this is the classic marketing equation, you want to have something that there's a lot of demand for but not much.

John Williams: Competition.

Paula Williams: Yeah, not much supply. So high demand, low supply, that's where the opportunities are. And the way that you tell that using Google's keyword planner is you look for words and phrases for which there is a lot of global monthly searches, a lot of people looking for that word or phrase, and not a lot of competition.

So that's an opportunity for you. And on our spread sheet we do some color coding and things like that, so if it has a really high global monthly searches we turn that green, if it has a really low competition we turn that green. And then the third thing we look at is the estimated average bid.

And that estimated average bid is just another way of looking at competition, because depending on how much people are actually paying hen they buy AdWords, which is a service that Google provides for that keyword. And it's not that we're going to buy keywords, we just want to see how much people are paying when they do buy an ad for those keywords.

Does that make sense?

John Williams: Well, it does to me. Hopefully it does to them, to our listeners.

Paula Williams: Mm-hm. Exactly so that's how you determine from the google key word planner where your list is currently is hanging out and also what words to use in your ads especially on line to get really good.

Search engine optimization.

John Williams: By the way, if it doesn't make sense to you, give her a call.

Paula Williams: [LAUGH] Yeah. A lot of folks throw up their hands at this point, and I don't blame you. Honestly, we did all of our own search engine optimization in 2009, and we did all of the search engine optimization for clients at that time and we even had a do-it-yourself package, as we said.

But since things have evolved we don't do a do-it-yourself product anymore, we do search engine optimization for clients, and I personally, meaning Paula Williams, don't do it anymore because there are people in the world that are much better at it for a lot less money than I'm willing to charge.

John Williams: And we hire those people.

Paula Williams: And we hire those people, so we don't even do a search engine optimization for our, or I don't do search engine optimization for ABC Ice Pages anymore. We hire that done. Because there are people who are so much better at it and because it's changing every day, and you really need somebody for whom that is their only job.

John Williams: If you look around a bit, you can find somebody that does it for a reasonable price and it has to be reasonable because they need to be on it pretty much every other day or so.

Paula Williams: Exactly, right. So keys to successful SEO. You want to choose words that your prospects are most likely to use, not what they should use.

John Williams: Oh, boy, is that a big difference?

Paula Williams: Exactly. This is a fight that we have with just about every client we have, right?

John Williams: We had a client that says he wanted to optimize for a particular set of keywords, and they didn't even show up in our searches.

Why?

Paula Williams: Mm-hm.

John Williams: Well, because that's what they should use.

Paula Williams: Right.

John Williams: Well, he's still trying to optimize for that and, of course, it isn't going to happen.

Paula Williams: Okay, and let me give you an example. There's a photographer who likes the term aircraft photography, but all of his customers use the term jet photography.

Now, he says that that's not accurate, because he photographs things other than jets, right? So, he calls it aircraft photography. But the thing is there are very few people who are actually looking for aircraft photography. They're all looking for jet photography, right?

John Williams: And once we convinced him, he was then amazed at the difference.

Paula Williams: Exactly. So, again, you have to meet people where they are, use the words that they use, and then you can teach them better, once they're clients of yours. [LAUGH]

John Williams: Right.

Paula Williams: So, it does no good to publish great stuff to an empty room. [LAUGH] So even if you're right, and you may be able to make the logical argument that people should be using this word, rather than that word, you're not **going to** win the argument on this side of Google AdWords or on Google keywords.

You have to do this yourself. All right, so online content. And we give some examples of how to judge the content on your site. A lot of people already have websites, blogs, and things like that. You want to look at how many people are actually visiting the articles and other things on your blog already, or on your website.

And whatever those most interesting things are, those are things you want to publish more of, right?

John Williams: Of course.

Paula Williams: Okay, so on our website in 2010, we published an article about pricing strategy, and we get a ton of traffic on that article. So what that says to me is that we should be publishing more materials on pricing strategy, right?

John Williams: Obviously.

Paula Williams: [LAUGH] Obviously. Right, and you can find that out from, again, our good friend Google, this time Google Analytics, which is another tool, another free tool that Google offers. And we do this for all of our clients as well. We do a report every month that says, here are the most visited pages on your site.

And so these are things that we probably want to do more of. And the least visited pages on your site are probably things that are not worth the time and effort, even though we may think they're important, nobody else does. [LAUGH] So, other than the things like the disclaimers that we have to have on the site, those are the pages that we really don't want to spend a lot of time and money doing.

Okay, so let me give you an example of how a blog post led to a sale. Actually, John, why don't you tell the story?

John Williams: Well, [COUGH] we noticed that our Alexa score was dropping off like somebody dropped an anvil out of an airplane. And we said, now, wait a minute, what's changed?

So, we ran a report and then come to find out that the site had been hacked, [COUGH] excuse me, with what they call a pharma hack, which means that now we have [LAUGH] links to places trying to sell pharmaceuticals.

Paula Williams: Right, like Xanax and weird stuff that have nothing to do with aviation marketing, right.

John Williams: And so we had our techies go into it, and try to figure out how to get rid of it. And they said, you know, there's actually a blog out here that tells you what you have to do. So, they sent me the email. I looked at it, and said, hm.

And then there was a link down at the bottom of the blog that said, this company will do this for you. I said, really? So, [COUGH] clicked on the link, went over there, and just did a quick once over the site, said, wow. We called them, they convinced us they were correct, we bought the product, four hours later it was done.

I mean, we'd have spent more time having our techies trying to do that, than have these guys do it.

Paula Williams: Exactly. So, this blog post, and a lot of people are concerned, they're afraid, especially people in consulting industries and things like that in aviation, they're afraid that if they tell people how to do something that people will go off and just do it themselves, they won't need to hire this consultant.

But that was not the case in this case.

John Williams: No, they spelled it out line by line by line, and which file, and which server, and everything, all the way down. And in which sequence you actually had to do it to affect a recovery. And then, what you had to do to get rid of the pages.

Paula Williams: Exactly.

John Williams: And it's step by step. And I just looked at it and said, you know, I mean, I got a data processing background, too, but no, it's not worth the time.

Paula Williams: Mm-hm.

John Williams: And then we bought the services and we decided to sign up for a year's worth, and it's cheaper than having anybody else worry about it.

Paula Williams: Exactly. So to be real specific, this is a company call Sucuri. We don't have any relationship with them, other than that we bought their product this week.

John Williams: Yeah.

Paula Williams: But they had an article on their blog called Understanding and Cleaning the Pharma Hack on WordPress, which is exactly the problem that we were having.

And rather than follow the instructions, what the instructions did was they gave us the-

John Williams: Information necessary to say we'll buy the product.

Paula Williams: Yeah, the confidence that they knew exactly what they were doing. And of course, there's going to be some set of people, if you publish an article that's a How to Do X, Y, and Z, there are some people who are going to take your instructions and run with them and do it themselves.

But there is going to be some subset of people that's going to read How to Do X, Y, Z that don't want to do it themselves, but now they know that you do. So, they're going to hire you as the authority on how to do X,Y,Z. And you've made a sale because of this blog post, right?

John Williams: And I'm quite sure they have processes that are automated to do all these things, and that's okay they should have.

Paula Williams: Mm-hm.

John Williams: But [COUGH] we didn't, and if we'd had our techies go do that, we would've paid more to get that done through our guys than if we'd just had this company do it.

In fact, that's what the tech suggested, we'd have these guys do it.

Paula Williams: Exactly, right. So, our tech found this article and suggested that we do that, and we did it. So, we're glad that they did that. But to bring that back to marketing for you, keys to successful online content.

Think from the customer's perspective, what did they want to read about? What problem are they having that you can solve, right?

John Williams: Absolutely, and that was a very good example of doing exactly that.

Paula Williams: Another thing you want to do is you want to publish consistently. That's another key to successful online content, because about every three weeks, if you haven't published something new to your site, you end up falling in your search engine rankings, because Google likes to serve the most current information first.

And if you haven't made any change to your website in about three weeks, they assume it's stale.

John Williams: No, don't wait for three weeks. Set aside some time during the week, probably toward the end of the week, and during the week make notes. I mean, use Siri on your phone or whatever, and make notes, and then, at the end of the week, write about it.

Paula Williams: Mm-hm. Another key to successful online content is to write great headlines. Nobody's going to read your articles if the headlines aren't good. And that article we just talked about actually was a pretty good headline, Understanding and Cleaning the Pharma Hack on WordPress. The things that we're looking for are something that's really specific, something that has the keywords that we'd be searching for.

Something that you know lends confidence, you can be kind of long with your titles, you want to be super descriptive, so great headlines are very important.

John Williams: A lot of writers will spend more time on the headline than they will on the article.

Paula Williams: Mm-hm. That's absolutely true-

John Williams: That very reason.

Paula Williams: Yep, a great article with a bad headline is not even going to even be seen, whereas a not so great article with a great headline Is going to be seen a whole heck of a lot.

John Williams: And you can translate that to websites. It doesn't matter if you got a quarter million dollar website, if it's not getting looked at by anybody, so what.

Paula Williams: Exactly, and then the last key to successful online content is to watch your numbers in Google analytics. Right and adapt accordingly, so if you've got an article that everybody is coming to. That's obviously a problem that a lot of people are having and that's something you can capitalize on.

John Williams: Ride Apollo onto that.

Paula Williams: Mm-hm. Absolutely. Okay, so next prospecting tool for online is.

John Williams: Video.

Paula Williams: Video. Right. Aviation marketing videos have gotten a lot more popular in the last year or two, because of the expansion of broadband.

John Williams: And video [COUGH] Does not mean necessarily you in front of a camera.

Paula Williams: Exactly. We're talking MP4 files, or MOV files, or anything that you can publish on the Web that shows moving pictures, you can do that with PowerPoint. You can do that with animation. You can do that with a slideshow of images. Lots of different ways of doing this.

John Williams: With appropriate voice-overs and comments along the way.

Paula Williams: Right. So we have a video on our front page that is kind of an introduction to our company. And a lot of people have remarked on the fact that they feel like they know us, because they've seen us on the video.

They've heard our voices. It kind of builds that credibility. When they pick up the phone to talk with us, they know what to expect. They know that we can explain things in a fairly simple way. [LAUGH] They know that sometimes we can explain things in a fairly simple way.

And they also know that we're fairly informal and friendly kind of people. And if that's people are looking for they're likely to find us and those are the kinds of people that we're most likely to have fun working with, right?

John Williams: Yep. Absolutely.

Paula Williams: Okay. So keys to a successful video.

John Williams: There's a lot of them but probably two of the major ones are pay attention to the sound, because if you're taking pictures somewhere like NBAA, guess what? There's a lot of racket going on there, and if you don't have the right types of microphones and mixers and things, the sound will not be something you want to listen to.

There's ways to get around that, and it's all, depending upon how much time you have. And you gotta consider lighting, and so forth. But bad sound is probably the worst thing you can get in a video. And then use something short, I mean don't get all carried away with 10 to 15 minute segments, do 1 to 2 minutes.

Paula Williams: Right. You actually saw something on the video today that you remarked on, that really caught your attention.

John Williams: This was a video form a company I subscribe to and what they did was, they actually had a guy on camera. So it was a guy on camera, and he did about a 10 second intro, and then stopped the video and had a blue screen and white letters.

It said whatever the question was, and then you had time to read that and think about it. And then he came on a video again, his face and so forth, in their studio, and answered the question with appropriate comments. That was about a 15 to 35 second video, and then he repeated the same thing all the way to about 5 minutes.

It never did get long.

Paula Williams: How long was the total video?

John Williams: Seems to me like 560 or something, 516.

Paula Williams: Okay, but it was broken up into-

John Williams: It was broken up by how they did it, but it wasn't really a stop start thing. You had to click on anything.

Paula Williams: Exactly. But if the guy had just been sitting there, talking and talking head for 5 minutes, you probably wouldn't have listened to the whole thing.

John Williams: Nah, I'd have got out of it.

Paula Williams: Okay, cool.

John Williams: And I hired these guys, I mean. [LAUGH]

Paula Williams: [LAUGH] Okay, so that tells you even if you've already made the sale you're still selling.

So even for things like your tutorials and other intro videos and things like that you want to make sure that you're using short segments. And also you want to make sure that you have really good sound, I think were the two things that we identified as keys to successful video, right?

John Williams: Yes.

Paula Williams: Fantastic, okay. Aviation podcasts!

John Williams: Have a good time.

Paula Williams: [LAUGH] Okay, I'll talk about podcasts. Okay. Podcast came up over and over again this year with some of the best marketing people in the business who had never really talked about

audio or podcast. And there's a couple of reasons that kept coming upv, one is that they're a very effective selling tool.

People seem to have a much longer attention span for a podcast than they do for text. So if you put those things side by side and we had this same material in a transcript, not very many people would actually read the whole thing. But a lot of people will listen to the whole podcast.

Because they can do that while they're doing something else like driving or whatever. The second thing is that podcasts are distributed through iTunes. So you are pretty much taking advantage of Apple marketing for you. Especially if you use those keywords when you put your podcast together and make sure that you are being found by people who have an interest in your product or service.

You want to be the one that people find when they go to iTunes, or click the podcast button in their car, and type in the term, for us is Aviation Marketing. For other people, it would be whatever their product or service is.

John Williams: Which is a good point, all the new, and I'm, don't know how far back.

But at least last year forward, all the cars have a podcast button in them.

Paula Williams: Exactly. So, keys to successful podcasts. This is a huge pain in the neck to set up-

John Williams: [LAUGH]

Paula Williams: The first time. There are some services like blog talk radio and some other commercial services that will do this for you, but the drawback of that is that they are putting their own advertising in your podcast.

And since your podcast is intended to be an advertisement for your company, you don't want them putting advertisements in that.

John Williams: So to do that without that you have to do every single friggin step yourself.

Paula Williams: Exactly.

John Williams: And it's painful.

Paula Williams: It takes, it took me several days, and of course I wasn't working on this constantly, but it took the better part of a week, to go through all of the steps to get, this podcast that you're listening to right now, setup with a, with a media host, the thumbnails, the descriptions, all of the stuff that you have to do to get it on your blog, get it publishing automatically.

All of those things, on iTunes, and Stitcher, and the other podcast outlets.

John Williams: But once you have one setup.

Paula Williams: Mm-hm.

John Williams: The subsequent podcasts are much easier to deal with.

Paula Williams: Exactly. So, and again, with all of these media, the key is also to publish consistently. So if you have a one episode podcast, it's not going to be very effective.

By about our fourth episode we started seeing a pretty big spike in traffic, and suddenly it went from you know a very small number, it went about four times that on about our fourth episode, and its gone pretty consistently higher since then. So I would say, you know, you want to plan a series of at least ten if you're going to do a podcast you need to commit to a series of at least ten.

John Williams: And then plan for the futures because everybody's going to have podcast button in their cars, and you don't even have to have a telephone, just push the buttons.

Paula Williams: Exactly, yeah, so if you can commit to doing this once a week, and for us this is not a bad way of going through.

Here's some of the material, and some of the things we're going to be talking about this month in our webinars, and some of the things we're talking with clients about. So it's work that we would do anyway, but we can just get together, huddle over the microphone and talk.

So it's not that hard once you've done it the first time. The other thing you can do is get a partner like ABCI. We do this for our clients where we set it up and then all you have to do is send us the audio file once a week and we'll take care of the rest of it for you.

So That is everything from scheduling your interviews to publishing your podcast. So depending on your level of service, that's an option for you, as well. Okay, next online prospecting tool.

John Williams: Webinars.

Paula Williams: Webinars. Exactly. So, why are webinars so popular?

John Williams: Well, they're sort of a step back from podcasts.

Paula Williams: Exactly. They're interactive media. In fact, they're more interactive than podcasts because you've got people on the other end of the. GoToWebinar session or whatever tool you're using and asking questions.

John Williams: Yeah well it's a step back because they have to take time out of their day and schedule and sit there and listen whereas in a car they can do it whenever.

Paula Williams: That's true that is true. So yeah webinars need to be live and you're expecting people to participate and so on, but you can also, answer questions live, and you can use audio, video, everything that you've got, to explain the answers to questions, and provide information, and everything else.

John Williams: Of course, you don't want to do any one of these things, you want to do them all.

Paula Williams: [LAUGH] Right, that's true. Okay, so keys to successful webinars. One is you want to advertise the heck out of them. Webinars don't advertise themselves. You know there's nothing like ITunes for For webinars.

[LAUGH] That we'll distribute this for you. You know you want to make sure that you're using email, and using other advertising venues, to advertise your webinars which are then, advertising your products. So it gets a little, convoluted, but-

John Williams: It works.

Paula Williams: It is definitely much more effective, than using Teeny tiny advertisements in a magazine is an example to drive them to a webinar.

There is no way that you could put the kind of information that you could include in a webinar in a teeny tiny advertisement in a magazine. So it really helps you maximize those dollars that you've spent on that advertising right?

John Williams: If, absolutely.

Paula Williams: Another thing is, you want to use interactive tools.

Good Webinar is the one we use. They add more features all the time where people can Where they can chat, where they can raise their hands. They've got polls. They've got handouts. They've got a lot of different tools that you can use,

John Williams: And you can record it, and you can get a transcript and send to people if you choose if they pay for it.

Paula Williams: Exactly. To make that work. One thing you definitely want to do is practice with your tools. There have been some incidents on live webinars, and if you are a frequent guest of our live webinars you are very familiar with the fact that things don't always work perfectly.

John Williams: No, and you have to be Ready, willing, able, and able to get around whatever happens, and keep the thing going.

Paula Williams: Exactly. I need to take a picture of the way that we set up for our webinars, because we are both in the same room, we've got two different computers, we've got dueling screens going on, a total of four screens-

John Williams: Mm-hm.

Paula Williams: Where we're looking at The presentation we're giving, the chat windows, the tools for time going by and all of the different things that we have going on.

John Williams: And run on a server network to see what everybody else sees.

Paula Williams: Exactly. So we can see if the slides are actually advancing for other people and not just for us.

John Williams: And we have had times when they don't just pass for everybody. [LAUGH]

Paula Williams: Right. Or if the sound goes out.

So all of those things, are things that you need to be aware of. And our way of doing that is a pretty elaborate setup.

John Williams: Well, but it has to be, otherwise you can't deal with issues as they come up, and you don't want to drop off in the middle of a webinar.

Paula Williams: Exactly, and again that's another service that we offer for our clients is to set up webinars for them so basically all they do is Skype in, or go to a meeting in, go to webinar as a tool of Citrix. Same as go to a meeting. So they just basically use their computer, dial in We facilitate the webinar for them, record the whole thing and take care of all of those things but if you're doing it yourself you want to make sure that you've got all the bases covered and that you have spent the time to make sure that all of those things are working right.

Okay last one I think. This is number six. Social media is our last tool that we're going to talk about today. ADCI publishes a guide to social media in the aviation industry. This is our first annual one. The reason we do them annually is [LAUGH].

John Williams: Stuff changes.

Paula Williams: Stuff changes. Yes. Everything changes. Every year there are new tools introduced. Once in a while one goes away. Once in a while one goes away, and the demographics of each of these tools changes pretty significantly. Like, three years ago Everybody was laughing at the idea of using Facebook for advertising in aviation and now there's a lot of companies using it very successfully.

The demographics have shifted to older. They've shifted to more male than female on a lot of the websites that we monitor, a lot of the social media Facebook pages that we monitor. Just Facebook has changed a lot. Twitter has changed a lot as well. It is a really great place to Get in touch with media contacts because it is so easy to search.

And a search capability is so fast and so granular that a lot of reporters use Twitter to find pictures, to find facts, to find pieces of data that they need for articles that they're working on.

John Williams: And if you're keeping up, Twitter's going to change again this year. They are expanding their 140 characters to somewhere between 140 and 10,000.

Paula Williams: Exactly. It will be interesting to see how that works. I hope they keep the search as fast as it's always been.

John Williams: Don't know, but that's just what I have heard.

Paula Williams: Right, the reigning king of social media and aviation has been for a number of years LinkedIn that's still true.

But LinkedIn is also changing, they used to have product pages on LinkedIn. They got rid of those and now they have highlight pages and they have company pages and groups where people can have group discussions and other kinds of things. So there's a lot going on in social media, and that's why we publish a guide every year.

So that's available on Amazon, or through ABCI, to get the whole guide. But just to summarize some of the keys to using successful social media. One is, don't publish ads to an empty room. You know, if you've got 10 followers or 100 followers, you're wasting your breath. You really want to build your audience first.

And the way that you build your audience is, you provide helpful information. You know, you can provide a fact of the week. You can do, like we do our Marketing Mondays, Webinar Wednesdays, Facebook Fridays, or Follow Fridays. Where we talk about marketing issues and also marketing news. We share information from our clients and from the aviation industry to make that more interesting and so on.

You have to think kind of like a magazine editor. What are your readers the most interested in seeing? Ask questions of the people that follow you, ask what people think. Or give them an A or B choice, which is your preference? You can get involved with some of the controversy in the industry, like user fees or drones and other things.

And if you take a position, somebody's going to respond [LAUGH]. So you have to think that through, but there's lots of ways to build an audience that are very legitimate. You want to just use those features. You don't want to ever buy traffic. Because you can always do that.

You can pay some of these companies that promise to find you 1,000 followers, or whatever, within 5 days for 100 bucks, or whatever the deal is.

John Williams: And you get pharma hacked.

Paula Williams: And you get pharma hacked [LAUGH]. That's not why we got pharma hacked. That was actually a vulnerability in our comment-

John Williams: Yeah, but Situation Somebody else paid them.

Paula Williams: In WordPress. Exactly.

John Williams: And this was. That's what they did.

Paula Williams: That's what they did, exactly. So there's somebody who's willing to pay bunch of people sitting in a room in some foreign country to click links all day long.

And that is not the kind of people that are worth anything to you. They don't provide insight into the topic, they don't add to the conversation, they don't buy your products. Which is really what it boils down to, right? One thing that I found that it is a lot more robust than I was ever expecting is Facebook's ad targeting.

If there was one tool that I think you should try this year, it's Facebook ad targeting. The reason is because you can spend very little money. You can spend $50 or less to do a test of this. And you can get very, very specific about the type of people that you're looking for.

By geography, by buying habits, spending habits. Do they have a type rating in this particular aircraft? Have they ever worked for this company or that company? Did they go to school at Embry- Riddle? I mean lots of things that really help define a really great audience for you. And it doesn't cost a whole lot of money, and you get really, really fast results.

John Williams: From a private person's perspective it's kind of scary. From a marketing perspective, it's outstanding.

Paula Williams: Exactly. [LAUGH] It's happening, it's just which side of the deal do you want to be on, right? Okay. So, wrapping up. Online prospecting tools. We talked about six of them, right?

John Williams: Yep.

SEO, which you now know is search engine optimization if you didn't already.

Paula Williams: Yep. Two?

John Williams: Content.

Paula Williams: Online content. Three?

John Williams: Videos.

Paula Williams: Four?

John Williams: Podcasts.

Paula Williams: Five?

John Williams: Webinars.

Paula Williams: And six?

John Williams: Social Media.

Paula Williams: Absolutely. Okay. So next week we're going to talk about offline or traditional media.

And we're actually going to talk about four of them. We're going to talk about events, magazine ads, postcards, and newsletters. So get the tips sheet. Once again, you can get 17 great calls to action. Which has been a really popular tip sheet, we're going to keep that one out there for another week.

Because a lot of people have really enjoyed that and have mentioned some things about it so that's great. Yeah, so go ahead and aviationbusinessconsultants.com. And go to the latest episode and you will see that download. So, thank you for joining us. Make sure you subscribe to our podcast on iTunes and leave us a review.

John Williams: And we'll be talking with you next time. Happy new year.

Music: [MUSIC]

Narrator: Thanks for joining us for Aviation Marketing Hangar Flying. The best place to learn what really works in sales and marketing in the aviation industry. Remember to subscribe on iTunes and leave a rating.

Did you know . . .ABCI offers Digital Marketing for Aviation companies?

Other Digital Marketing Topics

Aviation Digital Marketing Glossary

Problems and Solutions

Marketing and Privacy – Mutually Exclusive?

Balancing marketing efforts with privacy concerns is something we discuss with every new client, and something that everyone involved with marketing or sales should consider carefully.

We recently spoke with an entrepreneur we met at a trade show.

"I just started a new business venture, and of course I want it to be successful. We have an innovative product and I need to do everything I can to get the word out."

I asked what his plans were for marketing his new business. He listed the "usual suspects" – a website, pay-per-click ads, magazine ads, trade shows, and so on; but complained that all of these venues were "so expensive!"

Since he was concerned about cost, I asked if it was likely that the target prospects for his demographic would be on social media.

"Well, yes, I've heard a lot about that, but *I'm not willing to go on social media. Just because I want to make a profit doesn't mean I'm willing to give up my privacy!*"

We didn't have time to go into the details that would be required to explain that using social media is not an automatic divulgence of all of the details of ones life!

Like many people, this man was confusing the medium with the message.

Families at the turn of the nineteenth century were afraid to have telephones installed in their homes and businesses because they were afraid that the neighbors, the government, and the competition would be listening in on every conversation. They quickly became more comfortable as they learned that the telephone only "divulges" to other parties the things you actually say on an open telephone line. (Before the NSA became involved, anyway!)

Granted, there is MUCH information shared by telephone that should not be, but that doesn't make the telephone at fault!

These days, privacy concerns about simply having a telephone installed in your office have been minimized, and it would be unthinkable to run a business without a telephone.

(It can be argued that cell phones have active microphones and tracking devices, but that's another story.)

The point is, these devices have limitations. Social media channels such as Facebook, Google Plus, LinkedIn, Pinterest and Twitter can seem creepy simply because many of the people who use these services tend to "over share" details of their lives that nobody finds interesting but themselves; but in an of themselves, the social media are simply communication devices, like the telephone. The content of the information shared is up to the parties on both sides of the conversation.

It's a great idea to have policies in place regarding what employees are allowed to share in any public forum, including trade shows, dinners with friends, telephone conversations AND social media.

Regardless of the media, here's our recommendation.

Things you should share.

Your photo.

The privacy concerns: You might argue that you're not photogenic, or camera-shy, or that you don't want your face to be stored in a database somewhere as a biometric identifier; but frankly, if you're running a business, you're a public figure. You probably have a drivers' license. You've probably been in a bank or an airport at some point. Like it or not, your smiling mug is probably already a matter of public record.

The marketing concerns: Who would you rather buy a product from – someone who stands behind a product publicly and personally, or someone who looks like he or she is hiding from customers? (Or someone else?)

From this profile photo, I might assume that this person does not want to be associated with his business, or does not want to be recognized for some other reason. (Maybe he's wanted by the FBI? In a witness protection program?) Either way, he's not my first choice of a business partner or	From this profile photo, I might assume that this person "stands behind" his company and his product. I also might recognize him as someone I met at a networking event. I assume he's open to discussing his product or service and I'd be more likely to call him on the phone or click a "contact" button to

vendor.	find out more.

Customer Testimonials and Reviews

These may include customer satisfaction surveys that customers gave you permission to share, or comments that people published on your social media pages.

- **The privacy concerns:** Naturally, we want to keep our "dirty laundry" to ourselves and resolve conflicts as privately as possible. We also don't want to share anything unless we have permission from the customer to do so.

- **The marketing concerns:** What customers say about us is much more credible than anything we might say about ourselves. And hopefully, most of these testimonials and reviews are favorable. But even if they're not, showing the public how you acknowledged a misunderstanding or problem and attempted to make it right will give new customers confidence in doing business with you.

Your Competitive Advantage

What do you do better than anyone else? Why should customers buy from you rather than your competition? Can you show the difference with a side-by-side comparison? A chart or graph? A product demo video? An interview with a subject matter expert or a celebrity? By all means, produce that material and publish it everywhere you can.

- **The privacy concerns:** Many people are afraid that if they show their competitive advantage, their competitors will use that information to improve their own offering. Well, that's the risk you take being in business! If your product is not actually better than the competition in a demonstrable way that is hard to replicate, it may be time to go back to the drawing board!

- **The marketing concerns:** Aviation consumers are very smart. In most cases, this is exactly the information they're looking for to make the purchase decision.

A bit of personality

We like doing business with people that we know SOMETHING about.

- **The privacy concerns:** Of course we don't want to share any personal, private, financial or sensitive details of our private lives.

- **The marketing concerns:** There are plenty of things that we can share that help people get to know us a little bit that don't compromise our privacy but are interesting, entertaining or funny.

My Starbucks Name. I have to say, the coffee was worth it.

Little snapshots of daily life in the office, in the hangar or workshop or on the ramp can provide a little bit of insight into your personality and give people a chuckle.

By not taking ourselves so seriously, we make potential customers feel more comfortable picking up the phone to talk to us.

Things Not to Share

- Anything you're not comfortable sharing. Any online media has the potential of being shared with ANYONE. Pretend you're standing in Times Square with a megaphone. Are you comfortable sharing this information with your grandmother, your kids, your competitors, and your ex-spouse?

- Deals or negotiations that are "in the works" and not public.

- Your "secret recipes." Anything about HOW you create your product or service and make it better than the competition.

- Any personal, financial or medical information.

- Anything that is NOT entertaining, educational, or interesting.

Whatever media you choose to use for your marketing, it's important to have a policy, to follow it yourself, and to educate your sales, marketing and customer service teams to protect themselves and each other while doing a great job of marketing.

A Quick Tip for Getting More Online Reviews!

Why are online reviews important for aviation companies?

Airline brokers, charter organizations, flight schools, consultants and other aviation companies are not like most retail companies.

A Quick Tip to Get More

REVIEWS
Online!

We know that.

Most of us aren't doing as many transactions as the Starbucks down the street, but reviews are STILL important to us.

Online reviews help our customers make the decision to choose us – because others did and are FIVE STARS happy they worked with us.

We've often said that things our customers say about us are MUCH more credible than things we say about our own company. People are more likely to believe other customers!

But many of us are uneasy about asking for online reviews, and many of the people who we ask for reviews are excited to do it but aren't sure how, and get distracted before they get the job done.

Unless we really make it REALLY easy for them. . .

For example, don't just direct them to your Facebook page, direct them to the form for completing an online review – if you're a Facebook user, try it here:

Leave us a review on Facebook here!

https://www.facebook.com/pg/marketingforaviation/reviews

And don't just direct them to your Google Local page, send them to the form to complete a review –

https://support.google.com/business/answer/7035772?hl=en

Here are five tips for helping customers write a review of Trip Advisor

https://www.tripadvisor.com/TripAdvisorInsights/w698

And these are just a starting place. Focus on one, two or three review sites – generally the ones that you use the most for marketing in other ways.

Also, you know how important testimonials are on your website and marketing materials as well.

Encouraging customers to provide them can be awkward or challenging for many reasons.

The Most Common Reason
Marketing Campaigns Fail

Many of the people who come to us for marketing advice do so only after having tried many campaigns that fail to meet their expectations.

Marketing seems so simple – all you have to do is reach the right people and let them know that your product is the best available solution to their problem, and of course they will make the most rational decision.

Unfortunately, it's not that simple.

It's my contention that more marketers fail for this reason than for any other reason: They simply underestimate the difficulty of their tasks at hand.

-Dan Kennedy

In the aviation industry, we like to think that our customers and their potential customers are intelligent, rational and courageous. It's very easy to underestimate the amount of time and effort required to get their attention, to present our case, to get them to agree with us that our product or service is the most rational choice, and to make a commitment and write a check.

The truth is that B2B buyers may feel that their very job is put at risk by every decision, every purchase, and every embrace of a new or different vendor. Even entrepreneurs or otherwise smart business owners or C level executives who are apparently used to decisively "calling the shots" need more convincing than we would expect before they part with their hard-earned capital.

What seems like a simple decision for an aviation-related purchase usually involves most (if not all) of the following:

- In depth research to find the right prospects (target market)

- Strategy to find the right communication channels and venues for advertising

- Hours of perfecting and polishing advertising messages

- Days, weeks or months of relationship and trust building

- Reams of information, including newsletters, product sheets, demo CDs, articles, social media "information snacks,"

- Many phone calls (sometimes 20+ separate calls over a period of time)

- Personal visits (at trade shows, conventions, your place of business, their place of business)

Without a measurable, results-oriented *system* to provide a road map to re-use, automate, measure and continually improve this effort; and skilled, trusted people doing the work at every level; marketing becomes prohibitively expensive. Companies typically give up too quickly on prospects. They don't meet their sales quotas or revenue minimums. Many can't sustain their expenses and they go out of business.

Our specialty is **Long Cycle Marketing**^{SM.} This style of marketing is particularly effective in the aviation industry; as well as other large-ticket, high-trust or complex products and services.

In exchange for high-quality information the prospect then begins a cycle of progressive, long-term, low-key, low-cost and educational contacts using a mixture of media, including social media, direct mail, email, video clips and other methods as determined based on the demographics of the target prospect. **Long Cycle Marketing** is designed to position our client as the knowledgeable expert and source of information on the topic, as opposed to being viewed as a salesperson or vendor.

The prospect is thus moved further along the sales process.

After the sale takes place, **Long Cycle Marketing** continues to nurture the relationship so that testimonials, referrals and resells become a natural consequence.

Of course, this whole process depends on publishing *interesting, high-quality, relevant content* that your customers enjoy reading or viewing. We develop and produce excellent articles, podcasts, newsletters, and video to educate your customers and prospective customers about the unique value you bring to the table.

Action Items

Be prepared to work! If marketing was easy, EVERYBODY would be doing it well and have plenty of customers.

Budgeting and Return on Investment for Marketing Expenses

"Why do we lose money on advertising? Why don't I see a return on investment for marketing?"

An aviation company executive, on the phone with us for the first time, was clearly exasperated.

He had spent thousands on a magazine ad, thousands more on an email campaign, and had yet to recoup his "losses."

"If advertising is an investment, where the heck is the ROI?" he complained.

I absolutely understand his frustration.

Advertising for new customers is an expensive proposition. Trade shows, magazine ads, direct mail, even email broadcasts take good money out of your budget that you won't see again for awhile. If you have an incomplete marketing system (or a "leak," or malfunctioning piece your marketing system) most likely you'll never see that money again.

No matter how good an advertising campaign is, everything else in your marketing system has to support it. Your ad should have a call to action that leads people (that see the ad) to your website or to call a phone number. If your website doesn't provide a good impression in the first few seconds, or if the person answering the phone is not an effective salesperson, most prospects won't continue. There are lots of options on the market these days and decision makers are reluctant to part with their capital.

Even if you DO make a great impression, chances are it will be weeks or months before the sale is consummated. Unless you have a great information delivery or "lead nurturing" system in place, chances are they'll forget about your fantastic ad and the fantastic conversation they had with you before the "stars line up" for the transaction – and they'll either get talked out of buying your product or will spend the money elsewhere.

It IS possible to achieve a positive ROI on marketing, but it takes a complete marketing system that protects your investment AFTER each advertisement.

A realistic ROI also needs to be calculated based on the **cost to acquire a customer,** the **length of your sales cycle**, and more importantly, the **lifetime value of a customer**. In the aviation industry in particular, all of these figures are probably higher than you think. But it's vitally important to know each of these numbers.

As a result of years of practice in the aviation industry in the trenches, we've developed **Long Cycle Marketing** to protect ours (and our clients') investments. It's designed to reduce the initial cost to acquire customers. It can shorten the sales cycle where possible by delivering high-quality information using appropriate, sometimes automated methods. Where the sales cycle can't be shortened, Long Cycle Marketing ensures that leads continue to be nurtured cost effectively. Most importantly, we remain in contact with current and past customers, who are your very best source of referrals, testimonials, and repeat purchases.

While most marketing companies focus on **Phase One,** we recommend spending only 50% of your marketing budget on Phase One Activities, and dividing the remaining 50% between Phase Two and Phase Three (depending on the amount of time your company has been in business and the number of customers you've served in the past, among other factors.)

Phase One is a necessary part of growing your company; therefore we recommend a mix of media in order to establish credibility and reach new customers. However, advertising to people you have no prior connection with is the least cost-effective form of marketing. Advertising experts acknowledge that marketing initiatives having to do with new customer acquisition frequently don't even achieve 100% return on investment (ROI.)

Phase one activities . . ." incur negatives; an expense, or more properly thought of, investment in securing a customer, just as digging an oil well requires investment before any oil can be withdrawn for profit."

- Dan Kennedy, GKIC Insider's Circle Marketing Letter, June 2013.

Phase Two activities occur once a prospective customer has taken some action, such as downloading an eBook or requesting an information package. These prospective customers have a much higher probability of engaging your services, and are a much better "bet" for marketing investments. We recommend developing high-quality materials to keep these prospects engaged during the time between first contact and the consummated transaction.

Your best return on investment will come from **Phase Three** activities. Customers who already know, like and trust you are far less expensive to "re-acquire" than new customers who have never heard of you. This is also your best source of marketing materials, since what customers say about us is much more trusted than anything we can say about ourselves.

Just Having a Social Media Account Doesn't Mean You're Doing Social Media Marketing.

Yes, and you also have a telephone. That doesn't mean that sales are pouring in.

Many of our clients are confused by the fact that, although they have set up a web page, a Facebook page, a Twitter account, a Pinterest account, a Yellow Pages ad, or whatever, they are simply not getting the results they want.

In most cases, they are confusing having a marketing *channel* with having a marketing *strategy*.

Simply having a marketing channel is not the same thing as using it in the most effective possible way. Just like that telephone on your desk could sit there unproductively for weeks, or could be used by your 15-year-old daughter to make calls to her friends, or to be used as part of a powerful sales strategy. Even getting a better phone with more buttons is unlikely to help, either. If you want to use your telephone to make sales, you have to use it to build relationships with people. You actually have to have a list of people you want to contact, and great information to tell them, or great questions to ask them.

Same thing with other communication devices, like websites, Facebook pages, or Twitter accounts.

Any communication device is only as good as the quality of the content it's used to carry, and who is on the other end of the line.

In many cases we find that although clients have already established a website or a social media channel(s), they are missing a crucial component (usually one or more of the following)

1. They have not established a strategy or measurable objectives for its use; (We collaboratively define and use SMART objectives – Strategic, Measurable, Achievable, Relevant & Time Bound)

2. They don't coordinate the use of this channel with the other channels and activities in their marketing system;

3. They aren't using tools or strategies that could make their time spent on this channel much more effective;

4. The channel is not performing adequately to meet their objectives. As an example, they are not engaging with the correct demographics, or the material they're posting is not framed correctly for the audience or the medium.

5. They miss opportunities by failing to coordinate with influential media channels and thought leaders in the industry who are always looking for new material for magazines, blogs, podcasts, TV, radio and other publications.

With any of our consulting packages, we include a consultation period. During that time, we will decide with you whether our system should supplement or replace any of the marketing channels and strategies you already have.   If something is already working, we won't interfere with it. If it could be working better, we will help you improve it. If it's broken or missing, we'll build you a new one.

Action Items

Simply being present on a social media channel is the same thing as having a telephone in your office. It doesn't mean that anyone is making calls or answering the phone.

The Secret of a Good Advertisement

The power of one . . . via AWAI (American Writers and Artists International)

Ken Segall was once in a brainstorming session with Steve Jobs, debating how many features to include in an iMac commercial.

Now, as a writer, you probably know that focusing on one idea is best. But for some reason, Steve wanted to include five points.

Another guy in the room, Lee Clow, crumpled five sheets of paper into balls and tossed one to Steve. Steve easily caught it.

Lee said, "That's a good ad."

Then Lee said, "Now catch this," and threw all five balls to Steve.
Steve didn't catch any.

"That's a bad ad," said Lee.

Do your marketing habits work for you or against you?

Great marketing habits are much more important than any particular marketing technique or activity.

Your net worth to the world is usually determined by what remains after your bad habits have been substracted from your good ones.

-Benjamin Franklin

We can debate all day about the best exercise program, but we all know that spending four hours at the gym one day a month will not make up for a twenty-nine days of missed or sketchy workouts, no matter how much we pay for a personal trainer or use specialized machines.

In marketing, as in exercise, a consistent routine trumps a really hard or expensive workout once in a while.

Getting and staying healthy depends more on frequency and diligence than on an particular activity.

And yet for some reason, when it comes to sales and marketing, we think we can ignore sales and marketing tasks and stay busy with the customers we have, until suddenly we lose a big client, or get toward the end of the year, realize we are not as close to our goals as we'd like.

We start buying ads, going to trade shows, and "dialing for dollars," driving our few prospects crazy with our persistence.

It doesn't work that way.

With an exercise program, you're more likely to get injured or sore by "overdoing it" if you fail to build good habits.

With a marketing program, you're more likely to damage your cash flow or your company's reputation if you fail to build good habits.

So, we advise clients to develop a routine that works for them. The fact that you have a routine is more important than performing any particular activity on any particular day, of course, so adjust to what works for you. But here's a model program we advocate:

Marketing Monday

There are always more things that need to be done than time in which to do them. Spend an hour each Monday planning and prioritizing your marketing system and your tasks for the week.

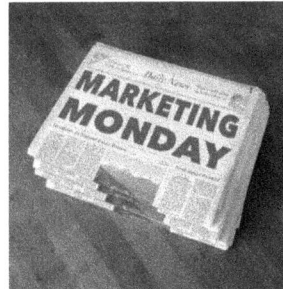

- Evaluate your progress toward sales and marketing objectives

- Determine where the weak spots are in your marketing plan. (The "leaks in your funnel," or the places that prospective customers tend to drop out of the process.) Work on strengthening the steps around the weak spots.

- Write blog articles or newsletters.

- Make sales calls.

Webinar Wednesday

Our Master Class Members invest time and energy to keep their sales at peak performance.   We suggest attending one webinar a week to keep learning and implementing new techniques and keep your skills fresh. Order lunch in one day a week, and use the time to get a great speaker or attend a webinar. ABCI has live monthly webinars on Wednesdays at 1:00 MST.

On the "other" Wednesdays, watch a recorded webinar instead!

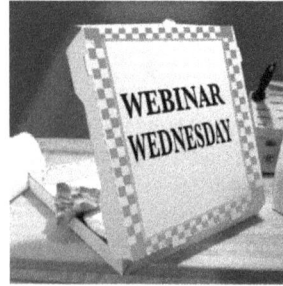

Facebook Friday

Sales and marketing are all about relationships. Everyone tends to be more relaxed on Fridays, so celebrate by spending some time on the "fun" parts of marketing-

- Research your top ten most wanted customers and partners on social media. Make comments and connections as appropriate.

- Reach out and make contact with any new people in your marketing funnel or on your top ten list(s)

- While you're on social media anyway, research your competitors!

- Post your site on ABCI's Facebook Page, and follow other aviation companies that post there.

We call this "Facebook Friday" because of the nifty alliteration, but really we mean ALL of the social media that are appropriate for your company – for you, this may include the NBAA AirMail, LinkedIn, Twitter, YouTube, or Pinterest.

(For the record, you're wasting your time in any social media channel unless a good number of your most desired customers, most feared competitors, and most important partners are using. Our rule of thumb is to check your Top Ten list – if most of them are present and active on a social media channel, it's worth spending the time. If not, check again in six months to a year, but for now you should spend your time connecting with those potential customers in other ways.)

There is no "magic" that can take the place of consistent, intelligent, honest work.

But we've found that having a great routine takes a lot of the difficulty and indecision out of the process. You can be a slave to your habits, or you can make your habits work for you!

Action Items

Routines can help you batch, organize, and get work done more efficiently.

The Almost Creepy Power of Data Analysis

The appropriately named chain store does an amazing job of targeting consumers based on statistical analysis. What does this mean for your marketing efforts?

In Forbes magazine on February 17, you may have read about how Target determined that a girl was pregnant and sent coupons to her home, surprising her family.

While some find the story creepy, and others alarming, the larger question for people involved in sales and marketing is this:

What are you going to do about it?

Some uses of this data analysis technology are intrusive and pose ethical questions, and may cause us all to doing our weekly shopping with cash (first ensuring that the bills are unmarked, of course) as a sales or marketing professional, the reality is that the technology to predict consumer purchasing behavior exists and is being used by your competitors.

Target statistical wizard Andrew Pole explained his methods:

As [his] computers crawled through the data, he was able to identify about 25 products that, when analyzed together, allowed him to assign each shopper a "pregnancy prediction" score. More important, he could also estimate her due date to within a small window, so Target could send coupons timed to very specific stages of her pregnancy.

Setting pregnancy aside and talking about aviation, there is no shortage of data.

There are scrupulous records kept by every aircraft in the U.S., and of aircraft in other jurisdictions by the regulating agency. There are records of ownership, maintenance, and even records of travel for instrument flight plans.

There are also records of pilots, A & P mechanics, and other licensed professions related to aviation.

There are numerous professional organizations, like NBAA, AOPA, NARA, and EAA that keep detailed records on their members, as well as results of surveys and other research.

The data is out there, the question is, which pieces of data can you get your hands on, that could be a predictor for a need for your product or service? Perhaps it's time to perform a bit of statistical wizardry of your own.

Action Items

Data analysis, like any other superpower, can be used for good or evil!

Aviation Business and Consumers Don't Buy the Sizzle. Why Content Marketing Matters

"People just don't seem to be responding. We have Facebook, we have Twitter, we're doing emails and postcards and ads, but we get no takers. I just don't get it."

When people send us samples of the current marketing they're doing, or when we research their companies online, we often find their marketing is composed of messages like these:

- "Like us on Facebook!"

- "Our product rocks!"

- "Our customers rock!"

- "$10 off on Product X!"

- "Photos from our Cookout!"

- "Our customer service rocks!"

Not bad for a start, and better than nothing. But a little lacking in, well, substance!

Jay Conrad Levinson's Monumental Secret of Guerilla Marketing – Secret Number 15 is this:

Sell the **content** of your offering rather than the style; sell the steak AND the sizzle, because people are too sophisticated to merely buy the sizzle.

This is true in the business-to-business space, and particularly in aviation!

Great companies don't sell products. They sell solutions to problems or opportunities to make their customers' lives better in some way.   That includes more than just a widget or gadget or piece of software, or even an airplane, as fantastic as airplanes are.

We get so attached to our products and services that we forget they are merely the means to an end to our customer. Our objective should be to provide a **better** means to that end. We need to be very well acquainted with your customers' objectives and problems. And we need to position ourselves as the best tool to reach those objectives and the best solution to those problems.

Without information and context, one gadget or widget or piece of software is just about the same as the other. But when it comes with *useful* information about why you need it, how to use it, and how it's different from the competition, this widget or gadget or piece of software has just become much more valuable.

We're all in the information publishing business. Like it or not, we need to provide our customers and prospective customers with conversations, stories, instructions, comparisons, text, pictures and video. In other words, content.

What makes great content?

Ann Handley & CC Chapman put it this way in Content Rules:

Share or solve; don't sell. Good content doesn't try to sell. Rather, it creates value by positioning you as a reliable and valuable source of vendor-agnostic information. Your content shares a resource, solves a problem, helps your customers do their jobs better, improves their lives, or makes them smarter, wittier, better looking, taller, better networked, cooler, more enlightened, and with better backhands, nicer muscles, and cuter kids. In other words, it's high value to your customers, in whatever way resonates best with them.

The key part of that thought – it's not about you. It's not about your company, or even about your product. It's about THEM.

One of our first activities with a new client is to help them develop an Editorial Calendar. We take a compiled editorial calendar from most of the major aviation publications and brainstorm connections to their company, product, service, and most importantly, customers. We want to enter that conversation that's already taking place in the aviation community and become vibrant, helpful, informative participants in that conversation.

Here are some ideas for creating substantial, helpful, fascinating content:

- **Listen before talking.** Do some surfing of your top 10 most-desired clients' websites and social media profiles. Or the magazines and blogs that your most-desired clients are likely to read. What do THEY talk about? Can you enter their conversation? (By commenting on their blog posts or discussions, re-tweeting their content, or posting it on your blog or newsletter with commentary?)

- **Brainstorm your ideal client's top 10 problems**, concerns and pet peeves. Write about the problem about which you can offer the most help.

- **Brainstorm your ideal client's top 10 aspirations and desires.** Write about the one that is the most relevant to your area of expertise.

- **Write about your clients.** Success stories are the very best marketing material. They show your concern and connection with your clients, and they show how your product or service solved a problem or improved a situation.

- **Write a Buyer's Guide.** People shopping for the product or service that you offer may not know what criteria they should be using to choose the best option. Write an honest, legitimate buyer's guide to help people decide on the best option for them based on the options available on the market.

- **Create a Video.** If you present at trade shows or do other types of public speaking, you have given the same presentation to live audiences and have refined it because of the feedback you get from your audience.   Produce that refined presentation as a video, and use the video as content on your blog, or send CDs to current and prospective clients.

- **Use current events, movies and other current stories.** Use the topics that people are already thinking about and apply them to your product, service or area of expertise whenever you can.

- **Add some personality.** Like posting the photos from your employee cookout, this helps people identify with you and feel like you're somebody they would enjoy working with.   Southwest Airlines is famous for this – they produce YouTube videos of retirement parties and other celebrations and really make their customers feel like insiders.

- **Show rather than tell.** Using examples, tables, graphs, charts, images, and even video is much cheaper than it used to be, and is usually much more effective at demonstrating a product, service or concept than plain old product specification sheets. (Which also have their place, but they can usually be improved upon!)

Building a better product than your competitor has always been the name of the game in business. That has evolved to the point where the name of the game these days is to provide a better solution than your competitor does. And that includes providing better content than your

Action Items

Sure, you may have a better product than your competitors. But do you have better *content?*

competitor does.

World's Most Under-rated Marketing Technique – Listening!

Are you spending too much time broadcasting and too little time listening?

The vast majority of companies spend entirely too much time, energy and money "putting their message out there" in proportion to the amount of attention to the actual living, breathing human beings that they are "putting it out" to. This results in a tone-deaf delivery at best.

We don't listen to the guy standing on the street corner with the megaphone. We tune him out so that we can listen to the friend with whom we're walking down the street.

To take this metaphor a bit further, we want to position ourselves as the friend walking down the street with our prospect, rather than the guy on the corner with the megaphone who is pointedly being ignored; or even resented!

How do we do this?

- **We spend time in the places our prospective customers spend time.** This might include conventions, trade shows, **SOCIAL MEDIA VENUES**, chat rooms, or networking events.

- **We listen first.** We know our prospective customer, and his needs or concerns. We read our clients' blogs and postings. We listen at networking events. We spend twice as much time reading as writing. In any venue, we take the time to listen first when we meet someone, before we start spouting off the benefits of our particular product or company.

- **We speak like a friend, adviser or helper,** rather than the loudmouth with the megaphone, clamoring to be heard. An occasional low-key sales pitch is fine, (everyone knows we're in business and have to make sales!) as long as it's in good taste and relevant to the particular prospect you're talking with and doesn't sound like it's addressed the general population.

- **We provide help when we can.** Cutter Aviation's FBOs help pilots, travelers and other professionals at the where they are located, whether or not they are customers. That reputation means they build relationships and are regarded as the "go-to" experts to solve problems and get things done. That leads to more business for them.

- **We maintain credibility.** We tell the whole story – strengths and weaknesses of our product or service. If it's not a good fit for a prospect's current situation, we say so. We don't advertise 50% off sales every week. That only insults the intelligence of the customer that made a purchase from us **LAST** week. Aviation is a small community full of very smart people. Exaggeration is not advisable. Even among salespeople.

Have a look at your current marketing system. For each activity in which you are putting a message out there, see what information you're taking in. Here's what we mean:

- **For direct mail, target your lists carefully.** Narrow it down to the smallest denominator so that you're speaking to a very specific group of people. A postcard that says "Mr. Williams, are you interested in selling or leasing your 2010 Skyhawk on profitable terms?" is much better received than a postcard addressed to "Dear Friend" (or not addressed at all) that says "SELL YOUR AIRPLANE NOW FOR CASH!!!!!" The technology exists to target very specifically and to personalize marketing pieces – failing to use this technology is perceived as indifference to the prospective customer – "I want your money but I didn't care enough about you to find out about the specifics of your situation or to use your name."

- **In networking events, ask about their business first before you tell them about yours**. We've talked about the importance of an "elevator pitch" or a concise way of explaining the unique benefit of whatever you're selling. But equally important is WHEN to deliver the elevator pitch. Show some interest first, and see if you can find a way to help the other person first before collecting another business card for your stack. The "elevator speech" is for use when you are asked – and you're more likely to be asked (and listened to!) if you've made it a point to get to know the other person first.

- **For blogs, tweets and social media status updates – read more than you write.** This is a great way to learn what they're interested in, what their concerns are, and what they may need at this very moment. We've made several sales resulting from a tweet or update that says "Who do you know that can help with my website?" or "How do get a new webpage listed by Google?" Being there right when they need help puts you in the best position to acquire a new customer.

- **On your website, remember that it's all about the customer.** They don't care what year you company was founded, or even particularly care what products or services you offer, until they know that you can help them. Frame the first few seconds of their experience from their point of view. Do you save them money? Help them stay legally compliant? Keep them safe? Help them serve more customers? Spell out the key benefit from a customer's point of view before you ask them to spend time learning about your products, services, company or yourself.

- **For email campaigns, honor opt-ins and opt-outs.** Email on a regular schedule – same day of the week or month, and use consistent headlines so that your readers can sort your emails and read them all at once when he or she has time, or have them go to a particular folder. Be sure that your email usually contains more useful information than sales pitch.

The interesting thing about listening is that it takes a lot less energy (and a lot less money) than nearly any other marketing technique. And yet many companies that say they are strapped for cash insist on shelling out good money to buy advertisements in magazines they don't read, banner ads on websites they don't frequent, and sales pitches they post to groups and chat rooms where they never read or respond to other people's posts. They're essentially buying bigger megaphones to stand on the street corner and spout a message that everyone is trying harder to ignore.

They're trying so hard to sell that they can't be bothered with the people they're selling to.

They are usually shocked to find out how much their sales improve when they start doing the one thing that costs nothing but time and attention – listening!

Action Items

In social media, active listening means responding to comments from prospects and customers, actively reading THEIR social media profiles and commenting appropriately.

Evaluating Specific Tools

Buying Advertising for Aviation Products & Services

Buying advertising used to be pretty simple. The choices were fairly limited and the audience was pretty well defined.

Selling a plane? The obvious choice was to list it in the big yellow **TRADE A PLANE** magazine (we're still subscribers and fans) using a cookie-cutter format. Even the words used to describe each aircraft were remarkably similar. Now even Trade A Plane offers online marketing packages.

Selling any aviation-related product or service? You could buy ads in one of about five aviation magazines, or you could show your wares at a trade show. Companies with deep pockets did both. That would pretty much cover the range of buyers of aviation products and services.

Now, there is a dizzying array of options for advertising.

Many aviation professionals are tempted to commit what we like to call **"random acts of marketing"** - aimless, unmeasured, potentially wasteful and reputation-harming marketing activities.

There are online and offline magazines, websites, Facebook, Twitter, webinars, and more. Magazine ads include QR codes or links to downloadable information packages. Trade shows have become more complex as well, with exhibitors making special offers and invitations in special "apps" on the smartphones of attendees strolling the aisles.

Time for some good, basic information.

Buying advertising is buying the attention of potential buyers.

Regardless of the format or medium of the advertising, the key factors used to make the purchase decision and how much to pay are these:

What kinds of viewers or subscribers will see the ad?   Are the readers of the magazine, attendees of a trade show or webinar, subscribers to the blog, "fans" of the Facebook page, or followers of a twitter account fit the demographics of typical buyers of your product or service?   Does the venue fit the profile of your product?   Selling shoe shine equipment for FBOs is more appropriate at NBAA than at Sun & Fun.

How many of those "somebodies" will see the ad? Magazines provide you with a media kit that includes circulation numbers and demographics.   With trade shows, we look at attendee numbers and demographics of attendees.   With websites, we look at Alexa traffic rankings, subscribers to RSS feeds, associated social media accounts, or Google Analytics. We also look at click through rate and participation of the online community. Do people actually engage in discussions and participate in some way, or do they just read a quick news item or look up information they need and click away?

This table shows a few of the key statistics (for comparative purposes) for a few of the advertising venues used for aviation products and services.

Website	Total Visits/Month	Facebook Fans	Twitter Followers
www.aviationweek.com	1,300,000	196K	148K
www.aopa.org	1,200,000	153K	52.8K
www.eaa.org	400,000	129K	39.2K
www.aviationpros.com	210,000	2,657	3,251
www.nbaa.org	130,000	41.6K	31.3K
www.thirtythousandfeet.com	30,000	N/A	N/A
www.avm-mag.com	2,000	N/A	18.9K
www.dommagazine.com	2,000	N/A	N/A
www.mromanagement.com	1,000	N/A	N/A

- **Traffic Rank** is a ranking of the most popular websites on the Internet. (#1 gets the most traffic, highest number gets the least.) This is determined by the Alexa system.

- **Indexed Pages** is the number of pages that the Google search engine "credits" to your site. Google sends more traffic to sites it sees as "bigger" and more extensive.

- **Linking Domains** are a measure that Google and other Search Engines use to determine how "important" a website might be. The more links to your site from others, the better.

How credible is the medium? Unless your company is as well known as Cessna, it's a great idea to "borrow" some credibility by associating your company with older, larger, or more renowned names and brands than your own. Advertising in Aviation Week or the NBAA website (www.NBAA.com) may be more expensive than advertising on Thirty Thousand Feet, (www.ThirtyThousandFeet.com) but it also adds a certain cachet that can help you sell more products.

How will you measure response to the ad? It's very important to use a "call to action" that describes what you'd like potential clients to do in your ad that includes a special phone number, link or code (here we go with those QR codes again!) so that you can measure response. Some effective calls to action, depending on the product or service could be:

- **"Call us today for a free consultation"**

- **"Download our online information package today."**

- **"Make an appointment before March 31 and receive a free gift."**

- **"Watch this two-minute video to see our product in action."**

You can evaluate the effectiveness of your ad and make decisions based on how many people follow the "call to action" using your special code or number.

Buying advertising is STILL pretty simple, but there are many more choices. Many of those choices are much more affordable than the options that were available in the past.

AMHF 0092 – Aviation Digital Marketing – Please Enjoy Responsibly!

This episode was inspired by another aviation marketing consultant, Rocco Cipriano of Aviation Marketing Consulting.   We've enjoyed several conversations with Rocco over the years and have even referred some business back and forth, so I don't know that we'd call him a "competitor" as much as a "respected colleague."

That said, we had to respond to a recent article on his blog – "Don't be Impulsive with Social Media Marketing."

While social media marketing does, by its nature, lend itself to impulsive decisions, Rocky uses a case study in the article that we wanted to counter with a few of our own. We'd also counter with our Rule #1 – "No Random Acts of Marketing."

Aviation Digital Marketing
ENJOY RESPONSIBLY!

We've seen much MORE harm done to companies by an impulsive appearance at the wrong trade show or an impulsive purchase of a print ad contract in the wrong glossy magazine that happens to be askew of their target market.

We also love Rocky's provocative use of this quote –

"Social media is like teen sex. Everyone wants to do it. No one actually knows how. When finally done, there is surprise it's not better."

AVINASH KAUSHIK

We agree. A lack of information plus an excess of impulsivity can lead to bad (or at least disappointing) outcomes. But we would argue that social and digital tools are just as safe and effective (and just as dangerous in the wrong hands) as print, direct mail, trade shows, or any other aviation advertising or marketing method.

Transcript of podcast episode:

Paula Williams: Welcome to Aviation Market Hangar Flying episode number 92. Aviation Digital Marketing, Enjoy it Responsibly. This one was actually inspired by our friend Rocky Cipriano, of Aviation Marketing Consulting, right?

John Williams: Mm-hmm.

Paula Williams: Okay, so I'm Paula Williams.

John Williams: I'm John Williams.

Paula Williams: And we are ABCI, and ABCI's mission is.

John Williams: To help all you ladies and gentlemen out there in the aviation world sell more products and services

Paula Williams: Absolutely.

John Williams: In this case, responsibly.

Paula Williams: [LAUGH] In every case, responsibly.

John Williams: [LAUGH]

Paula Williams: No "random acts of marketing," right?

John Williams: Exactly.

Paula Williams: Okay, so if you would like to reply to this episode or any other, you can use the hashtag #AvGeekMarketing, and we will do our best to find and reply to every tweet.

Of course, you can also comment directly on our blog, or in any other way that you'd like, send us an email If you'd like it to be confidential. Anything you like, we love hearing from you, right?

John Williams: Absolutely.

Paula Williams: Okay so, the big ideas today are we're going to do a case study of what to do with a $10,000 marketing budget.
We are going to hopefully emphasize the point that aviation digital marketing is not a universally successful item, it's not a magic button. It's not an easy button, it's not anything like that. In that we agree.

John Williams: And not a silver bullet.

Paula Williams: With Mr. Cipriano. But where we disagree is that we do think that it is a very powerful component of a great marketing program and we're going to give some examples of how that could work, right?

John Williams: Absolutely.

Paula Williams: Okay, so let's start with our inspiration. We thought this was a fantastic blog article because it gets attention, right?

John Williams: [LAUGH] It got yours.

Paula Williams: It's controversial, and it gets people talking about it. So good job Rocky, you've got this, you got your competitors talking about this on a PodCast. So what are the chances of that?

John Williams: [LAUGH]

Paula Williams: [LAUGH] All right, and actually in aviation there are very few what I would call true or pure competitors, where one person is tooth and nail against another person and their locking horns over the same customers. And I think that's true of us in aviation marketing as well.
Every aviation marketing company has its own specialty, and its own flavor, and its own style. And there's plenty of business out there for the rest of us. We're all competing against the Madison Avenue weirdos, right?

John Williams: As a matter of fact, we have recommended Rocky on various occasions and he has recommended us on various occasions.

Paula Williams: Absolutely, so there is nothing but love here between us and actually we thought this was a really great article. It just caught our attention and got us talking and we thought you know, we really need to talk to our customers about this, as well. So first of all, the headline, right?

John Williams: [LAUGH]

Paula Williams: Or the tagline. It starts off with a quote. Don't be impulsive with social media marketing. Totally agree with that. And then the quote, social media is like teen sex. Everyone wants to do it. No one actually knows how, and when it's finally done, there's surprise that it wasn't better, right?

John Williams: [LAUGH]

Paula Williams: That's too bad.

John Williams: [LAUGH]

Paula Williams: Very sad. Anyway, in the article, once he's got you rooked into reading it, which that does very well.

John Williams: Exactly.

Paula Williams: He has a hypothetical in there, and this is a great hypothetical. And I think everybody should run hypotheticals in their marketing, what if we did this and we got that result?

And he's doing a wonderful job of outlining the results you should expect, the benchmarks that you may set for yourself in a marketing plan, and so on. So let's say I run a six-month $10,000 advertising campaign for a client in trade publication reaching their target audience. Assume this campaign reaches 100 leads and a client closes 10.

The cost per new customer acquisition is $1,000. Great job on defining that right? Okay, and then he goes on to explain a social media program in which it's going to cost more and do less good, okay? So this is where we get the gloves out.

John Williams: [LAUGH]

Paula Williams: [LAUGH] Okay, it is more complicated than print versus digital, right?

John Williams: Yeah.

Paula Williams: And I think it's fantastic that you're setting a budget. I think that you're setting a time frame and you're setting an expectation of how many leads you're going to pull in, in that amount of time, right? So getting 1,000 leads is a great goal and spending $10,000.

Getting 1000 leads and closing 100 of them.

John Williams: Hey, that's not what he said.

Paula Williams: That's not what he said?

John Williams: No.

Paula Williams: Let's go back.

John Williams: He said getting 100 and closing ten.

Paula Williams: Getting a hundred and closing ten. Well that's a reasonable goal as well.

John Williams: See?
Everybody got to keep you on track here.

Paula Williams: [LAUGH] Getting 100 and closing ten. This is why you're the CFO right? 100 and closing ten. But it works with any marketing math you want to use here. We'll use that math. Okay, Rocky your numbers are accepted and verified by Mr. Williams okay? Carrying on, print verses digital.

John Williams: Actually, I would wager to guess that you use a little bit of both print and digital no matter who you are.

Paula Williams: Absolutely, the first thing I want to point out, is that every medium has it's pros and cons, right? Trade shows are fantastic, and they're kind of the king, [LAUGH] the reigning, traditional royalty of aviation marketing.

Are the results measurable? Usually, depending on how you do it. Does it target people who are looking for what you're selling? Usually, depending on whether or not you pick the right shows. The Concepts that we're talking about here, can you virally spread your appearance at a trade show from one person to the next?

John Williams: [LAUGH]

Paula Williams: No, it only works on the people who are actually physically in the room, right?

John Williams: Right.

Paula Williams: Does it last forever? No. It's just while the show is going on, and whatever follow up you do for that particular event. Does it target people who are ready to make a buying decision.

Not necessarily people who are going to that show are going to that show for any number of reasons, not necessarily because they want to buy a new widget, whatever that widget is? right?

John Williams: Exactly, and they're mostly doing research.

Paula Williams: Exactly.

John Williams: And when you hear of large sales made an aviation trade show, those are all put together, advanced and done for publicity.

Paula Williams: Exactly. Are the results visible this week? No. The results that you hear about at trade shows, like John said, had been talked about for weeks, months, or years ahead of time. They are one of the more expensive versions of advertising in the aviation industry.

John Williams: Of course.

Paula Williams: But they can also be very effective. Now, if we take this same table and we look over at the one, two, three, four, fifth column in print ads and look at those same criteria, right?

John Williams: Yeah.

Paula Williams: Are the results measurable? Possibly, only if you put in a good call to action, right?

Do they target people who are looking for what you do? Maybe, if you pick the right magazine, but then again, these aviation magazines are going to people every month. So not necessarily at the time that they're looking for what you're selling.

John Williams: Precisely.

Paula Williams: Okay, or are they virally spread from person to person.
You could argue that if I see an ad in a magazine, I might pass it to John and say, John, I want one of these. [LAUGH]

John Williams: But that's not viral, that's all a one-to-one.

Paula Williams: Exactly. So the chances of it being spread from person to person are slim. Does it last til it's removed? No, you do an ad in a magazine, it gets thrown in the recycle bin the next month.

John Williams: And that's done.

Paula Williams: Yep, absolutely. Does it target people who are ready to make a buying decision? Not necessarily, once again, they come out every month.

Are the results visible this week? No, absolutely not. There's a lead time on magazines and-

John Williams: At least 30 days, roughly.

Paula Williams: Yeah, it depends. When the magazine comes out, sometimes you can get a call the day that it comes out so.

John Williams: Mm-hm.

Paula Williams: That's a possibility.
How expensive are they? We put them in the three dollar sign category.

John Williams: [LAUGH]

Paula Williams: Because they're in the $1,000 or more for almost any publication in the aviation.

John Williams: Yeah, that'll only get you an eighth to a quarter sometimes.

Paula Williams: Exactly. And how effective are they? We put them as moderately effective.
So that's fantastic. And then, if you look at the digital media, search engine optimization and social media, we're kind of lumping those together as aviation digital marketing, right?

John Williams: Mm-hm.

Paula Williams: That's fair?

John Williams: Sure.

Paula Williams: Okay, so search engine optimization has its pros and cons, and social media also has its pros and cons.
So the ideal thing is to really cover your weak spots by using more than one form of advertising, right?

John Williams: Absolutely.

Paula Williams: Okay, so any campaign that you put together, you've got pros and cons. So let's talk about the pros and cons of print ads. The pros are that it's very respected, it's a very traditional media.

You can use that borrowed credibility. If you get an ad or an article mentioned in Aviation Week, you can put that Aviation Week logo on your website and say, As Seen in Aviation Week! , right?

John Williams: Yep.

Paula Williams: That's cool. The cons are the cost of it, and also the fact that aviation publications have been proliferating like nobody's business in the last few years, right?

John Williams: And a lot of times, what they will do is they will look at their target demographics. And then, if they're not selling enough, they will give away some so that they can say they got so many out there.

Paula Williams: Right, so their subscription numbers aren't what they used to be. Their circulation numbers aren't necessarily what they used to be.

John Williams: Right.

Paula Williams: And some of that circulation may be inflated because they're offering very low cost subscriptions. We often get advertisements for aviation publications for a dollar a month or ten dollars a month or free just by proving that we're in the industry and-

John Williams: We don't prove it. They see that we are.

Paula Williams: Yeah, exactly.

John Williams: And they send it out to us so we're surprised sometimes at some of the stuff we get.

Paula Williams: Exactly. So some of the people that are getting your print ads are not the same quality that they were five or ten years ago.
Which is not to say, once again, the pros aren't worth it in some cases, right?

John Williams: Right.

Paula Williams: Okay, so let's talk about pay per click, which is probably the shadiest of the aviation digital marketing stepchildren, right?

John Williams: Well, Google would love to hear you say that. [LAUGH]

Paula Williams: [LAUGH] Exactly.
It is fast. Okay, this is the fastest way to get an ad to the right people. If you set up your targeting right, and you have somebody who knows what they're doing. You can have an ad out there in 45 minutes, from the time that you have your first conversation with someone that knows what they're doing.
Or if you know what you're doing yourself. And that really is the kind of the heroin aspect of this, [LAUGH] Or the sugar rush aspect. This is a family show, right?

John Williams: Yeah.

Paula Williams: We're here talking about sex and drugs [LAUGH].

John Williams: [LAUGH]

Paula Williams: Anyway.

John Williams: All we're lacking is rock and roll.

Paula Williams: Exactly. We need some rock and roll in this podcast. So yeah, they are super fast. And if you have an event or a training program or something like that and you've got one last seat to fill, there is nothing that can beat to market a pay per click ad, right?

John Williams: Exactly.

Paula Williams: And when I'm saying pay per click, that can be Facebook, that can be LinkedIn, that can be Google AdWords. That can be anything where you're paying money to a digital media to post your ad right now, right?

John Williams: Next.

Paula Williams: Okay, so the cons are that they are expensive for popular keywords.

So there are really good reasons to do these. But we don't recommend that you do these as a regular daily doing business kind of way of going about things.

John Williams: Yeah, I mean, we've done research before and we've seen aviation keywords as expensive as $2,639 per click.

Paula Williams: Yeah, I mean that's insane.

John Williams: Who would do that?

Paula Williams: Yeah.

John Williams: Unless you're selling something for half a million bucks, I mean.

Paula Williams: And have a close rate of one out of two, or something insane like that. So if you know what you're doing, pay per click can really be a very valuable tool in your toolbox.
But it is definitely a sledge hammer that needs to be used very carefully.

John Williams: And every time a research says Steven known keywords that we're familiar with are going up in price.

Paula Williams: Right, it's more every time, it's getting frightening. Okay, so let's talk about Facebook, all right?
Facebook has numbers that you wouldn't believe nowadays. There's lots of places on the internet that are telling you what numbers of people are on Facebook. You can say, but I sell to serious people who don't use Facebook, like John. [LAUGH]

John Williams: Watch it now.

Paula Williams: Chances are the people that buy your product or service either are on Facebook and may not advertise that fact.
Or they know people who are on Facebook. And somebody's going to throw this in front of their nose like I do with John all the time saying, look at this thing on Facebook. And they've got coworkers or kids or somebody who's going to throw Facebook under their nose, if there's something that's very targeted to them.

John Williams: But the bottom line is this is how the individual or a small firm can have access to the term everybody uses is big data.

Paula Williams: Big data, or artificial intelligence.

John Williams: Yeah.

Paula Williams: Both.

John Williams: They have both there. And you have to get into it to figure out how to make it work to its best advantage.
But they do have it and they have some very nebulous instructions. [LAUGH]

Paula Williams: Right, so and the really cool thing about Facebook is it's probably the very best way for people who are not in the advertising industry. Or who are not in Fortune 50 or Fortune 10 companies to have the resources to do things like targeting behaviors.

You're at Oshkosh and you want to target only the people who are at Wittman Field right now. There is no other way to do that besides Facebook that I know of.

John Williams: And as far as serious people, we have sold everything from software to jets on Facebook, so I don't want to hear the serious crap.

Paula Williams: [LAUGH] Absolutely, so I guess you could target the people on Wittman Field by having somebody tow a banner around the field.

John Williams: [LAUGH]

Paula Williams: But-

John Williams: With the drones.

Paula Williams: With a drone, there you go. So that's using AI and it's using technology and everything else. But the easy way to do that is with Facebook.

And to set what they call a geotagging or a geolocator on your ad, saying you only want to advertise to people who are within a certain location, right? Okay, also re-targeting people who have visited your website, you want to re-target them using Facebook. That's really cool. So there's lots of things that you can do to target people who exhibit certain behaviors.

Who are probably more likely to see your ad and act on it because they are at AirVenture. So, they're going to drop by your booth, or they have been to your website before so you know they are interested in your product or service. So you're not wasting money on people who aren't, right?

John Williams: Right, exactly.

Paula Williams: Cool, the cons are that it is not-

John Williams: For those of you that are watching this, she types like I do. That is by, not bv. [LAUGH]

Paula Williams: By some, exactly, okay, fine.

John Williams: [LAUGH]

Paula Williams: Actually, what happened is, I didn't make the text box long enough to cover the little tail of the y.
What is that called, the hangy thing on the letter?

John Williams: Yeah, the anchor or whatever, I don't know.

Paula Williams: Yeah, okay, anyway, that is not seen as credible by some. So some people are not going to respect your Facebook advertising as much as they respect your ad in Aviation Week magazine.

John Williams: But the number of people who don't see it as credible is reducing daily.

Paula Williams: Exactly, so it really depends on the content and the targeting and a lot of other things. So how do you know what you want to advertise in? The only way that you can tell what's working for you is to look at your last year's results.
This is our last year's results.

John Williams: [LAUGH]

Paula Williams: Where did our customers find us, right? And most of them found us on our website, blog, or podcast. And unfortunately, we don't differentiate between our website, blog, or podcast, because many people use different media to access that same material, right?

John Williams: Yeah, it would be kind of interesting and long and drawn out to try to [LAUGH] –

Paula Williams: [LAUGH] Yeah, to figure that out.

John Williams: Differentiate that.

Paula Williams: Right, so anyway that's the big blue section, and that is 44%. The people that bought something from us last year found us on our website or blog.

A smaller amount than that found us on Google. A smaller amount than that found us on LinkedIn, then postcards, then Internet in general. And this is just what people tell us when we ask them, how did you find us, right? 3% found us at an NBAA education session, 3% on Twitter, 2% on Yahoo, [LAUGH] 2% on Facebook.

I suspect that's going to be bigger this year than it was last year. 1% on YouTube, 1% at an Aviation Pros show. This was actually two years ago, I apologize. 1% on email, and 1% in our online webinars, and 2% miscellaneous. In other words, they didn't remember how they found us, right?

John Williams: [LAUGH]

Paula Williams: Okay, so once you have this pie chart and you've been keeping track for a number of years, you have an idea. But even so, a lot of the people that found us through our website or blog found that website or blog through LinkedIn, you know what I mean?

John Williams: Mm-hm.

Paula Williams: It gets messy because people find you more than once. And they also will only remember the last contact they had with you, so.

John Williams: Guilty as charged when I talk to other people when I try to buy as well, so.

Paula Williams: Exactly, [LAUGH] now, this is a graphic that's been floating around the Internet for a number of years.

And there are a number of people who take issue with it in a number of different directions, either saying that the source is not credible, or it's too many or too few or whatever. But it's been quoted by everybody from Zig Ziglar to results.com to HubSpot. So we're going to use this to prove a point.
Whether or not you agree with the data, you probably agree with the fact that most people don't do enough follow-up. And most people don't do enough advertising to sell a product or service. It takes a lot more than once to qualify, well, to get somebody's attention, to get them to take action, to enter your system as a qualified lead, and to get the attention of one of your salespeople, right?

John Williams: Mm-hm.

Paula Williams: Okay, and what it says, for those of you that are just listening, 48% of salespeople never follow up with a prospect. 25% of salespeople make a second contact and stop. 12% make a third contact and stop. Only 10% of salespeople make more than three contacts, and so on.
The bottom line is, 80% of sales are made on the fifth to twelfth contact.

John Williams: And this is not in aviation, this is in retail.

Paula Williams: Retail, right, so in our experience it is worse than that.

John Williams: [LAUGH] Yeah.

Paula Williams: Depending on the product or service, and the larger and more complex the product or service, the more touches it's going to take.

So in a lot of cases, it'll take 20 or more contacts to make a sale. And those might be that they saw an ad, or they read an article, or they talked to your sales guy, or they got an email or, or, or, or, right?

John Williams: Yeah, as a matter of fact,

John Williams: We were trying to buy something for our home, once upon a time. And I was having this conversation with the saleslady. And she's, no, no, no, that's not true. And I said, really? This is the fifth contact with you.

Paula Williams: Right.

John Williams: [LAUGH]

Paula Williams: And this is something we wanted.

John Williams: That's right, this is something we wanted to spend money on. And she got so upset, she wouldn't call us back. So we went with a different company.

Paula Williams: [LAUGH] We're not trying to be difficult, we just have questions. And we rescheduled a couple of times, and things happened and everything else.

But we bought from someone else, and it probably took her five, six, seven, eight contacts. And that was just for drapes, right?

John Williams: That was just for drapes, yeah.

Paula Williams: Something simple. So if you're selling aircraft maintenance software or something that is more of a time and money commitment on the part of the person making the purchase, you can expect to be in this conversation for a really long time.

And you're going to have to expect that you're going to have to provide a lot of marketing information, a lot of advertising, a lot of contacts to get where you want to go.

John Williams: And you just as well like the people you sell to, because even after you make the sale, you need to keep in contact for subsequent sales.

Paul

a Williams: Absolutely, okay. So you want to do something that is cost-effective to contact people multiple times, right, or for them to find you multiple times. So if you do things that allow you to do multiple contacts, you can adapt as you go. And if you're doing something digital, you can see the results of each of these contacts.

So for example, I put on a screen a screen from our Facebook Insights. And it basically shows some of the Facebook posts that we've had in the last week or two. And you can see how many people saw it, how many people responded to it, by either clicking on it or sharing it or commenting on it or so on.
So I take the ones that worked the best, we make more like those.

John Williams: [LAUGH]

Paula Williams: We take the ones that did the worst, and we make less like those.

John Williams: Mm-hm.

Paula Williams: And so we can measure different things, like time of day, like headline, like the image that goes with it, like the message, like the offer, and so on.

And by testing, we can make this better over time. If you do something where you can only afford to do it once, twice, or three times, you really can't adapt to, well number one, you may not get the data back. Number two, you may not be able to adapt quickly enough to make that really worth the money, right?

John Williams: Yeah, exactly.

Paula Williams: Okay, so the good news is that with aviation digital marketing you get more than one shot to advertise to people. You're going to have to advertise to people more than one time. The good news is also that you can use more than one media, right? Nobody says you have to use one thing or another.

Page			Total Page Likes	From Last Week	Posts This Week	Engagement This Week
1		NBAA	45.5K	▲ 0.1%	33	938
2		AircraftMarketPlace: Ev...	7.9K	0%	3	9
YOU 3		Aviation Business Cons...	5.2K	▲ 0.2%	15	59
		Keep up with the Pages you watch.	Get More Likes			
4		AviationPros.com	2.9K	▲ 0.2%	25	3
5		Perfect Landing Media, ...	2.6K	▼ 0.2%	0	0
6		BDN Aerospace Marketing	2.6K	0%	9	24
7		Aviation Marketing Con...	1.6K	▲ 0.2%	2	0
8		Applied Composites En...	1.6K	0%	2	6
9		Greteman Group	1.4K	▲ 0.1%	10	47

John Williams: No, you can use more things and many times.

Paula Williams: Right, and our curmudgeonly mentor, Dan Kennedy [LAUGH]

John Williams: [LAUGH]

Paula Williams: Says, diversity equals stability, right?

John Williams: That's what he says.

Paula Williams: Okay, so if you have a great ad or a great message or a great article or something like that, you can adapt it to multiple different platforms, right?

So if you have something that is a great offer or a great story, you can do that as a press release if there's something newsworthy about it. You can make a postcard, you can put it on social media, in several different formats. You can do search engine optimization, create some content on your website about that item.

And do search engine optimization to get other people to link to it. Do all kinds of things to make that reach a number of different people in a number of different ways. So if you've got a great ad, article, any piece of content that you want to use, you want to recycle and repurpose that in a number of different ways, right?

John Williams: And printed could be one of those ways.

Paula Williams: Exactly, lots of ways to do that. Printed materials there's lots of options. Website there's lots of options. Social media, lots of options. If you have a podcast or know somebody who has a podcast, there's lots of options. [LAUGH] Webinars, lots of options there, right?
So amateurs put one hook in the water at a time, right?

John Williams: Yep.

Paula Williams: Professional people, professional marketers put multiple hooks in the water at any given time and they're a lot more likely to catch a lot more fish, right?

John Williams: Absolutely.

Paula Williams: Okay, so let's get back to the $10,000 case study.
Okay, $10,000 and our goal is to get as many qualified prospects as we can for that $10,000. And one of our options is to, and the one that Rocky suggested is print advertising. So if we look at these four publications and three out of the four have a quarter page ad is $3,000 or more.

Now granted nobody pays rate card, everybody negotiates. [LAUGH] You know, but.

John Williams: But this is also from two years so it's more expensive now.

Paula Williams: [LAUGH] Exactly, so there's a couple of things wrong with this. Number one is that nobody pays rate card. The second thing is that it is from a couple of years ago so it's probably gone up.

So we'll stay those things are a wash. So let's say $3000, to make the math easy, $3000 times 4 is $12,000. So we've already exceeded our budget but-

John Williams: And that's only for quarter page.

Paula Williams: Right, to make that reasonable, let's say it's $12,000 for a quarter page. Or let's say we can get a one full page ad for $10,000.

John Williams: Yeah, but that means either four issues or one issue.

Paula Williams: Exactly, so those are our options. We can do one ad and spend our whole budget, right?

John Williams: Yep.

Paula Williams: That's an option, and it might work.
But your chances of getting 100 qualified leads out of a single contact if they've never heard of your company before are slim and none. If that's the only marketing that you do in that six months, and in this hypothetical, we said let's say we have a six-month period in which we're going to spend $10,000, this is one option.

Okay, another option is we'll be generous and say that you've negotiated four quarter-page adds for $10,000. It's a possibility. So you've got four ads in the same magazine for $10,000. Also an option, you may or may not get 100 qualified responses for four ads within six months. Our experience is probably not.

John Williams: Yeah.

Paula Williams: People tend not to be that responsive to print ads, it's not quite that successful. I've never heard of anybody getting 25 qualified leads from one advertisement, right? Because the goal is 100.

John Williams: Yeah.

Paula Williams: You're doing the math for me, right?

John Williams: Well, yeah. Especially in aviation.
There are other things where you might, but in those cases you'd need more than that to make it worth your while.

Paula Williams: Absolutely, once again, that's four quarter-page ads. An alternative would be to do ten articles or press releases, for $10,000. And then you would only need to get ten to qualify leads from each of them in order to get to your number of 100, right?

John Williams: Yeah.

Paula Williams: And that's a lot more likely, I think, because when you do a press release, it is seen as, people have a different category in their brain for an article than they do for an advertisement, right? So they see an article in one of these magazines.
And often when we do press releases we find something newsworthy to say about a client, or a product, or an offer. And we'll get picked up by maybe three or four different, for each article we would get picked up by at least one usually. Aviation publication or financial publication, or whatever it is that we're targeting.

John Williams: I don't know that we've ever had one that low.

Paula Williams: Right, but we usually get at least somewhere in the neighborhood of 50 to 100 pickups in credible publications, maybe not all would be your target.

John Williams: Well, I know, but I don't think we've ever done low enough to be just one aviation publication.

Paula Williams: [LAUGH] Yeah. Exactly.

John Williams: [LAUGH]

Paula Williams: So you get mentioned in several different magazines in each of those articles. If you do ten articles, chances are you're going to be mentioned by some of these magazines more than once. You're going to be mentioned, possibly, in your local newspaper. You're going to be mentioned, possibly, in digital media, like the Aviation eBrief, and so on.

John Williams: And, you need to be clear. Ten articles, that's not in one week, right?

Paula Williams: No, ten articles within six months or you could do it in ten months. Our usual scenario is one article a month. I don't know that I'd recommend in six months because that would be kind of fast.

But one article a month for ten months is reasonable and I think that's a lot more likely to get your 100 prospects.

John Williams: Yeah besides I mean you need to be looking ahead. You don't just go out and spend ten grand, expect something to happen in the first four, five months.

Paula Williams: Right, that's true.

John Williams: I mean, in aviation, if you do, then maybe you've figured out how to do antigravity.

Paula Williams: [LAUGH] Something. Yeah, if you're selling antigravity units, I guarantee you're going to have a lot of interest. So-

John Williams: [LAUGH]

Paula Williams: If you have one, talk to John.

He really wants to get into that. To be honest here, these are not going to be all print publications. In fact, most of them are going to be online publications because most of these articles have an online version. They're going to pick you up in their online version.

But then of course, you can link to that in your emails. You can link to that in your social media. You can send that in emails to interested customers. And you can print those in PDFs and send them to people. There's lots of things that you can do.

John Williams: Yeah, because every time we get any publication, we get a link back to exactly where, and how and what it looks like. And we give those to our clients.

Paula Williams: Right, absolutely. Okay so that's one option is to do ten articles or press releases, then you have, as we talked about, ten more opportunities to adapt.

You can see which ones get the most response, which get the least. Every time we do this we'll look at the last one that we did and say, did this work, did it not work, what are we going to change? Once we have three, we get really good at seeing what worked, what didn't work, what we can change.

John Williams: Yep, they put a real fine point on it.

Paula Williams: Exactly.

John Williams: Not to put too fine point on it.

Paula Williams: [LAUGH] Exactly. Okay, to put an even finer point on it for $10,000, you could do 40 social media ads. So that would be ten months of our social media program which is about four ads a month in that category.
And once again, those are going to be targeted, those are going to be using the media that your customers are likely to use most. And we're going to be using some of those features, like geotargeting, or retargeting, so people who have visited your website and other things.

John Williams: And have used Facebook.

Paula Williams: Yeah.

John Williams: You can get so granular down to. Well, I'm probably overstating, what they have for breakfast every morning?

Paula Williams: I don't know if they have an algorithm that-

John Williams: [LAUGH]

Paula Williams: Would figure out what you had for breakfast in the morning. You have to [LAUGH]

John Williams: But you, hey, have very granular-

Paula Williams: Right.

John Williams: What you're targeting.

Paula Williams: Okay, and you might say, okay, well, my customers don't use social media

Paula Williams: BS, okay, we do surveys every year that show that a great number of aviation professionals do use social media of some kind. And John will tell you I don't use social media.

But John will also tell you that he does use Facebook. Or he does use LinkedIn, sorry. [LAUGH] Slander, my goodness. John does not use Facebook, but he does use LinkedIn, right?

John Williams: Yep.

Paula Williams: Okay.

John Williams: I do LinkedIn, it's been a good thing, actually.

Paula Williams: Right, and I have seen you look at things on YouTube before.

John Williams: Perish the thought.

Paula Williams: Perish the thought, [LAUGH] exactly. So those are things that you can look at. Twitter is actually used more often by other journalists, and things like that, then by customers. So, there are reasons to use it and reasons not to. We'd have to talk to you individually and figure out what would be the best media for you and what would be the best targeting for those media.
Right?

John Williams: And we can help you figure that out actually, down to very good reasoning.

Paula Williams: Exactly. Okay and from that same survey, you might say, well that's all lower level people. You know that's not Founders and C Level Executives and things like that. That's all the interns and kids and weirdos, right?

John Williams: No.

Paula Williams: No! [LAUGH]

John Williams: In work?

Paula Williams: Yeah, 40%, almost 40%, 39%. Don't exaggerate, Paula. I told you a million times, never to exaggerate.

John Williams: Mm-hm.

Paula Williams: 39% of the people that responded to our survey were Founders or CEO Level Executives, that said that they do use social media of some kind, right?

John Williams: Yep.

Paula Williams: Okay, and of those, how often do you log into any social media? 58% said more than once a day. Every time we do this survey, this light blue section gets bigger.

John Williams: Well, what's interesting and we say log in.

Paula Williams: Mm-hm. Maybe it's how many times do you reference-

John Williams: Well, no, no, no, no, no, no-

Paula Williams: Yeah.

John Williams: Because, no. Because once I decided to put the LinkedIn app on my phone, every time you touch, it would be considered log in.

Paula Williams: That's true.

John Williams: And I just wait til the possible red indicators on it and I touch it.
So every how often that happens is what I do.

Paula Williams: Yeah and a lot of people get alerts from social media, and they respond to those alerts. So that would be a time-

John Williams: But that was only LinkedIn, because it's the only one I do and it's a problem.
Averaged over a month, probably close to once a day.

Paula Williams: Okay, so you would be in the purple category.

John Williams: Yep.

Paula Williams: The 28% that do about once a day.

John Williams: Mm-hm.

Paula Williams: Okay.

John Williams: And that's just one social media. So if you've got three or four it's going to put you in light blue, automatically.

Paula Williams: Yeah. And I more than make up for your-

John Williams: [LAUGH]

Paula Williams: 28% because I log in to social media very often, right. Okay. So that's social media. Let's say that you, instead, do 10 months of search engine optimization. Okay? What you can expect from 10 months of, you say, well, what good will ten months of search engine optimization do for you?

John Williams: Well, now, this presupposes that you have a decent website.

Paula Williams: Yeah, exactly.

John Williams: [LAUGH] Because we have some that don't.

Paula Williams: Right, and if you don't have a decent website, and you may want to spend that $10,000 revamping your website, And we would certainly give you that advice before we take your money for search engine optimization, Because we're not going to sell you something that's broken, [LAUGH] right?

John Williams: Yeah, some of these $9.95 for a month websites are made with stuff that you just can't go in And tag keywords that put stuff in it without a major rewrite.

Paula Williams: Exactly. So that would be like selling you a $10,000 paint job on an airplane that has no engine in it.

John Williams: We don't do that.

Paula Williams: Exactly. So what search engine optimization does is it helps people find you. And as we talked about earlier, most of the people that found us last year that bought from us, found us on Google. Or at least that was a pretty big percentage.

Most of them found us on our blog or podcast. But there was a fairly large number that found us on Google. And I would suspect that a lot of people that found our podcast and so on, found it on Google, right.

John Williams: Very likely.

Paula Williams: Okay. So, a lot of people, especially in business-to-business, they're looking for something in particular, are going to go to a search engine and look for aircraft maintenance software or avionics.

A certain type of avionics, especially, because they're looking for something very specific and particular. So, search engine optimization can really do a lot of good for you and 10 months is, people ask, well, what can that do? Here's an example of a site that we did search engine optimization for 10 months.
And we got them over 40% more traffic over the previous 10 months. And the other nice thing about search engine optimization is that it lasts for a long time. So when you have a good site that's performing well and you've got good backlinks and everything else, those tend to stick around.

Even though Google does change its algorithm so you may need to touch this up three or five years later, you are going to continue to get good results for quite some time. This is not like pay-per-click advertising where as soon as you stop paying it stops being good, right?

John Williams: No, not like that. These are people that are interested in your product or service because that's what they're looking for.

Paula Williams: Exactly, you can't get more specific than somebody who's looking for ADS-B compliance or King Air.

John Williams: Yeah and there you go.

Comparison with competitors

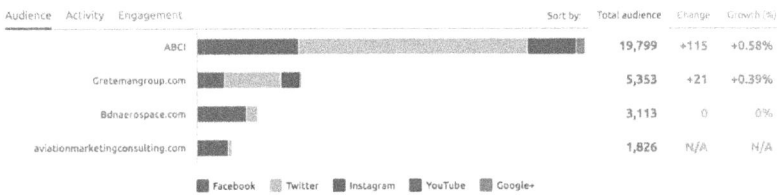

Audience Activity Engagement	Sort by:	Total audience	Change	Growth (%)
ABCI		19,799	+115	+0.58%
Gretemangroup.com		5,353	+21	+0.39%
Bdnaerospace.com		3,113	0	0%
aviationmarketingconsulting.com		1,826	N/A	N/A

Facebook   Twitter   Instagram   YouTube   Google+

Paula Williams: Yeah, exactly. Those are people you really want to talk to if that's what you sell.

Okay, so yeah, 10 months of SEO is a good option. So what we really recommend rather than print media, spending that $10,000, if that's all you have to spend for six months, use a variety of media. This would be a recipe that would depend on a number of things.

Who your customers are, what your competitors are doing, and a lot of other factors, but we'd probably recommend some recipe that looks like this. Maybe in this case, six press releases, four months of social media, four months of SEO, and two postcards. That would be a really effective package that would help your ideal customers see you everywhere.

And it is so much more credible when they see you in a magazine and then see you in their Facebook, And go to your website and then you've retargeted them, so that they see you when they log in to Facebook, and then they get a postcard from you.

And then they see another article two months later. That is so much more credible than just a single ad, right?

John Williams: Or even three ads.

Paula Williams: Or three ads, or four ads, that are all in the same place. And also, you can adapt. So as you can see, as we learn from doing those press releases, or that social media, we're adapting to what your customers respond to and not what they don't, right?

John Williams: Yep.

Paula Williams: Cool, all right. So once again you get more than one shot. You can use more than one media. Diversity equals stability. And I think you have a much better chance of getting those 100 qualified leads out of a wide variety of things that includes digital media.

John Williams: I'd be willing to bet that you get, well, it depends obviously but five or six months additional versus I would think, at least double to triple.

Paula Williams: Yeah, absolutely. And we are not against print. If you had $20,000 to spend, then we probably would advise you to get those four ads in a print publication, plus a variety of digital media.
And press releases, right?

John Williams: An integrated marketing plan.

Paula Williams: An integrated marketing plan, absolutely. So for more about the various advertising methods, you might check out Episode 28 of our podcast, Print Versus Digital-Round 1, [LAUGH] and Episode 29, Print Versus Digital, Round 2. In one round, print wins. In one round, digital wins just to-

John Williams: [LAUGH] You gave it away.

Paula Williams: I did give it away but you don't know which is which. There you go. So subscribe to our podcast, Aviation Marketing Hangar Flying on iTunes, Stitcher, Google Play, or wherever fine podcasts are sold. And please do.

John Williams: Podcasts aren't sold.

Paula Williams: No, they're given away.

John Williams: Okay, see?

Paula Williams: There you go.

John Williams: I'll keep you straight.

Paula Williams: And please do leave us a review. That really helps other people find us and get good information about aviation marketing, and not be running off doing random acts of marketing, right?

John Williams: Absolutely.

Paula Williams: Okay, so, yeah, enjoy it responsibly and have a great week.

John Williams: Yep, that's it.

Paula Williams: See you next time.

John Williams: See you next time. Ciao.

Is Twitter Worth The Time for Business-to-Business Sales? A $250,000 Case Study

"Twitter is great if you're a rock band or a cupcake shop, but isn't it kind of a waste of time for "real" businesspeople?"

This was not the first of our clients to express something like this. Most of our clients sell to businesspeople, not teenagers. They sell airplanes, parts, consulting services – expensive things that aren't bought on a whim based on a 140 character "tweet."

Or are they?

Gary Vaynerchuk's book The Thank You Economy includes a reference to the sale of a $250k phone system based on a relationship that started with a response to a tweet by Avaya's global managing director of Services and Social Marketing Paul Dunay.

On average, Avaya interacts with a couple of dozen customers through social media on a weekly basis. By listening, the team also comes across **sales opportunities**. In fact, 58 characters of a simple Tweet started the relationship with a potential customer.

"shoretel or avaya? Time for a new phone system very soon," the Tweet read.

"In less than maybe 15 minutes, we had seen it and figured out what the heck to say to this guy," Dunay said. "I wrote back, 'We have some highly trained techs who can help you understand your needs best and help you make an objective decision. Give me a call.'"

Dunay referred the gentleman to a business partner, and **13 days later, they closed a $250,000 sale**. At the same time, the new customer's follow-up Tweet went out: "...we have selected AVAYA as our new phone system. Excited by the technology and benefits..."

"**We were there. We were listening. It pays to listen**," Dunay said. "I can't say we hit 100% of the conversations where we've wanted to be, although it's probably 60–70%. But on our brand name, it is 117%. We're on every one of those."

When it comes down to it, Twitter is just another communication device. Does having a phone ensure you'll make sales? Not at all. But most companies would find it difficult to close deals without one. Having a Twitter account does not ensure that you will make sales either. It all depends on how you use it.

But one thing we can assure you – you will make no sales on Twitter if you don't have a Twitter account, or if you don't use it well.

Conclusion –

Action Items

Twitter is most useful if you attend trade shows or want to communicate with the media.

(Or, of course, if your Top Ten most wanted customers or most feared competitors are active on it!)

A Means to an End

Five Marketing Tasks you can Accomplish with Social Media Tools

In a **recent article** we mentioned that social media is simply a tool to be used to accomplish certain tasks, and that disliking Twitter makes about as much sense as disliking a socket wrench.

If you have a task to accomplish, and a social media tool is the easiest, cheapest and most effective way to get that task accomplished . . . what's the problem?

Well, we received a lot of questions since then. They mostly boil down to this:

"What kind of tasks could I accomplish using social media tools?"

Here are a few of our favorites:

1. Research your Top Ten most wanted customers.

You should have at least ten "future customers" that you are pursuing at all times- and you can ethically "stalk" them by observing what they publish in social media. Follow their accounts, read what they write, and comment when appropriate.

This is also a great resource to learn about a prospect before a meeting or sales call. (There is no excuse, in this day and age, for a "cold" call – you have plenty of research tools at your fingertips and can customize your reason for calling!)

Best tools for this task: LinkedIn, Facebook Company Pages

2. Plan your Trade Show Appearance.

It's expensive to travel to trade shows, but it's also a "target rich environment," to quote Top Gun. There is no excuse for wasting a spare moment. Use the show's official hashtag (#OSH15, #NBAA15) to discover competitors, customers and prospects that will be attending, and to connect and arrange times to meet for coffee or dinner or just to drop by their booth. .

Best tools for this task: Twitter, Instagram

3. Find out more about your current customers.

Enter a list of email addresses and you can get detailed reports on the demographics of the people that "like" your page on Facebook, or that visit your website, or serveral other variables. Best tool for this task: Google Ads Manager (Note – you can use a free account and don't have to purchase any ads.)

Relationship Status

Self-reported data from people who list a relationship status on Fa...

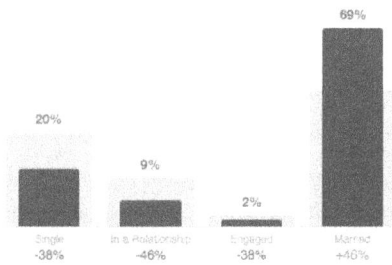

Single	In a Relationship	Engaged	Married
20%	9%	2%	69%
-38%	-46%	-38%	+46%

Education Level

The highest level of education reached based on self-reported dat...

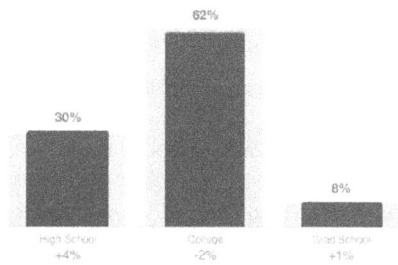

High School	College	Grad School
30%	62%	8%
+4%	-2%	+1%

Job Title

Likely industries where people work based on self-reported data on Facebook.

Job Title	Selected Audience	Compare ▾
Veterans (US)	14%	+213%
Military	20%	+159%
Installation and repair	14%	+112%
Farming, fishing and forestry	9%	+107%
Government Employees	17%	+106%
Construction and extraction	16%	+101%
Transportation and Moving	22%	+93%
Protective Service	7%	+92%
Cleaning and maintenance	8%	+88%
Architecture and Engineering	10%	+70%

See All

Best tool for this: Facebook Ads Manager, Twitter Ads Dashboard

4. Advertise an Event to specific groups.

Want to advertise an event for to licensed CFIs in certain zip codes in Texas?   No problem!

Best tool for this task: Facebook Events + Ads Manager

Note: We also recommend that you acquire a targeted list from AirPac or JetNet and send postcards about your event if time & budget allows. An additional media compounds the effectiveness of your advertising.

5. Educate prospects and customers.

ABCI and many of our clients sell products and services that aren't as simple as a socket wrench. We need to let people know what it is, why they want it, what the alternatives are, and how to use it properly. At the same time, we simply can't get our casual prospects to spend hours poring over a manual. So, a "tip of the week" or "Did you know . . ." series of information snacks can be very helpful to increase sales, improve customer satisfaction, and reduce returns and chargebacks.

Best tool for this task: Any social media that your customers and/or prospects use!

Any powerful tool has risks associated with it. It's important to know how to use them properly and take safety precautions.   In the case of social media, it's necessary to take many of these precautions (i.e. monitoring the reputation of your company, your product(s) and your brand) whether or not you personally are an active social media user. Whatever you and your employees do, you cannot control the actions of your customers and competitors on social media – so it pays to watch what they do.

Action Items

Twitter is most useful if you attend trade shows or want to communicate with the media.

(Or, of course, if your Top Ten most wanted customers or most feared competitors are active on it!)

Conclusion

Social media is simply one tool in the marketing toolbox.

Many of the misconceptions about social media come from our haphazard and casual use of it in our personal lives, as well as sensational news stories about the MIS use of social media.

By nature, social media lends itself to wasteful random acts of marketing.

But in the hands of a skilled practitioner, this tool CAN be incredibly powerful!

We look forward to hearing about YOUR use of social media! Give us a call at 702-987-1679, or shoot me an email at paula@AviationBusinessConsultants.com

GROW YOUR BUSINESS
CONNECT WITH US!

Addendum – ABCI Data

Do aviation professionals really use social media? The best way to tell you may be to show you our own results.

Visits to ABCI's website from various sources:

Social media came in third, after organic search and direct.   There is some argument that social media also improves the performance of other sources of traffic as well, since the search engines do take social media activity associated with a website into account when determining which pages to serve first.

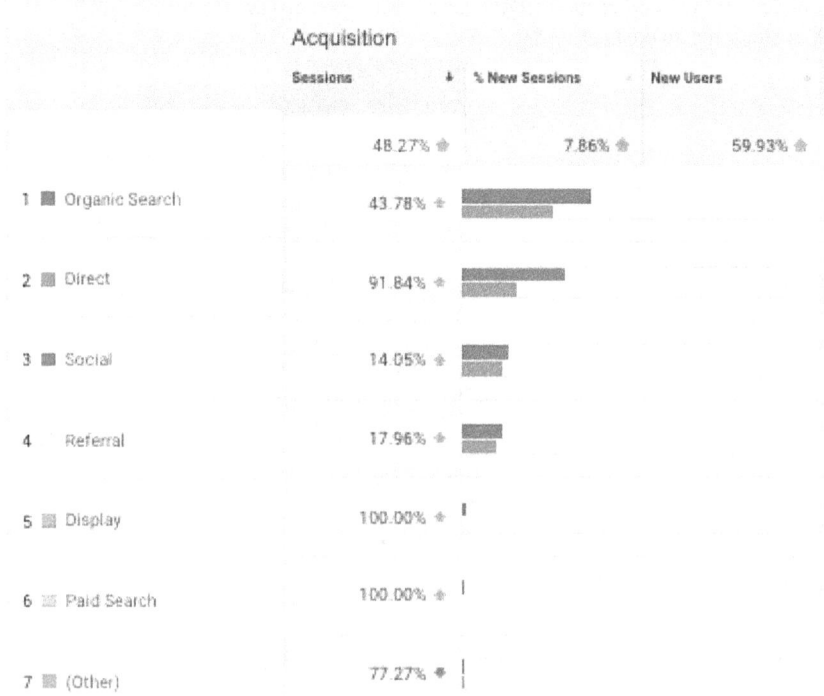

	Acquisition		
	Sessions	% New Sessions	New Users
	48.27%	7.86%	59.93%
1 ■ Organic Search	43.78%		
2 ■ Direct	91.84%		
3 ■ Social	14.05%		
4 Referral	17.96%		
5 ▦ Display	100.00%		
6 ▦ Paid Search	100.00%		
7 ▦ (Other)	77.27%		

Of the "Social Media" category, we like to see the total numbers. To figure out whether a visit was "high quality" or not, we like to see how many pages per session they visited, and how much time they spent on the site.

This would indicate that LinkedIn generated the most visits, but Facebook had higher quality visits.

Social Network	Acquisition			Behavior		
	Sessions ↓	% New Sessions	New Users	Bounce Rate	Pages / Session	Avg. Session Duration
	14.05% ⬀	4.35% ⬇	9.08% ⬀	1,038.05% ⬇	38.47% ⬇	19.32% ⬇
1. LinkedIn						
Oct 30, 2015 - Nov 29, 2016	1,981	70.57%	1,398	81.32%	1.39	00:00:52
Sep 28, 2014 - Oct 29, 2015	1,691	72.03%	1,218	3.67%	2.60	00:00:51
% Change	17.15%	-2.02%	14.78%	2,118.01%	-46.56%	2.11%
2. Facebook						
Oct 30, 2015 - Nov 29, 2016	1,783	55.64%	992	67.25%	2.70	00:03:32
Sep 28, 2014 - Oct 29, 2015	1,155	55.15%	637	11.17%	4.61	00:03:23
% Change	54.37%	0.88%	55.73%	502.09%	-41.45%	4.32%
3. Twitter						
Oct 30, 2015 - Nov 29, 2016	520	65.00%	338	54.04%	1.87	00:00:45
Sep 28, 2014 - Oct 29, 2015	897	67.22%	603	4.01%	2.89	00:01:10
% Change	-42.03%	-3.31%	-43.95%	1,246.46%	-35.24%	-35.65%
4. Google+						
Oct 30, 2015 - Nov 29, 2016	40	17.50%	7	32.50%	3.28	00:04:24
Sep 28, 2014 - Oct 29, 2015	52	59.62%	31	13.46%	2.63	00:01:16
% Change	-23.08%	-70.65%	-77.42%	141.43%	24.31%	247.98%
5. Instagram						
Oct 30, 2015 - Nov 29, 2016	18	77.78%	14	83.33%	1.22	00:00:16
Sep 28, 2014 - Oct 29, 2015	0	0.00%	0	0.00%	0.00	00:00:00
% Change	∞%	∞%	∞%	∞%	∞%	∞%

Prospects in our "House List"

It's interesting to see how people come to find us for the first time, (website traffic and the origin of people of visited our websites) but what is MORE interesting from a marketing point of view is how many of these people actually provide us with contact information.

- In our case, people give us their contact information in one of several ways:

- They request an appointment for a consultation.

- They request a tip sheet or other "lead magnet" from our website.

- They call our office.

- They provide a business card at a trade show or other networking event.

A caveat - over the course of a relationship, people may make contact with us multiple

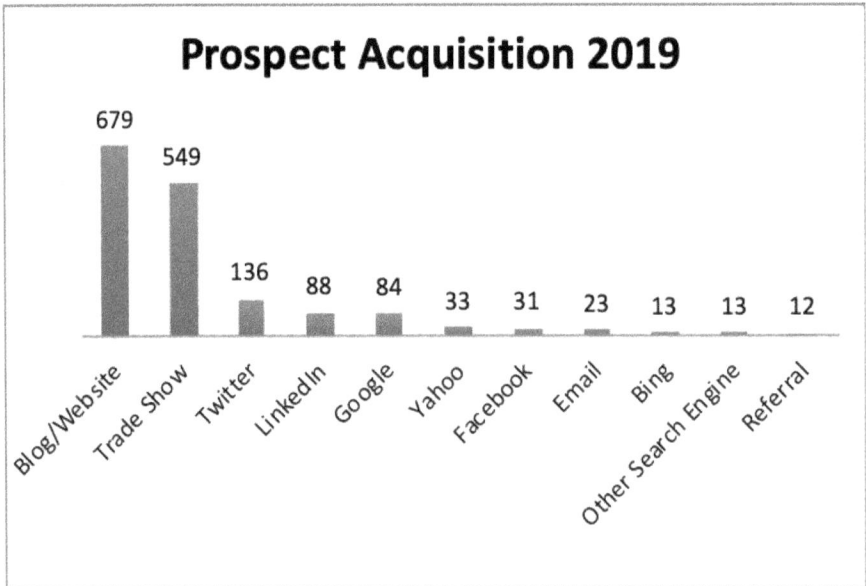

Prospect Acquisition 2019

Source	Count
Blog/Website	679
Trade Show	549
Twitter	136
LinkedIn	88
Google	84
Yahoo	33
Facebook	31
Email	23
Bing	13
Other Search Engine	13
Referral	12

times, but only the first contact is recorded.

ABCI Customers

Of course, the ultimate value of all this marketing is for people to become customers themselves.

Our "sales cycle" is currently about 8.5 months, which means that much time elapses between the time they first make contact and provide their contact information and when we actually receive money for a service.

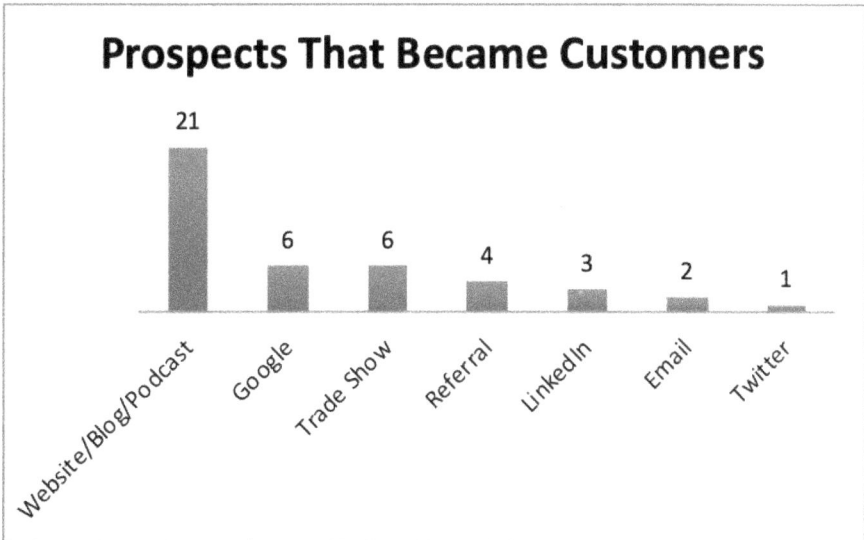

Prospects That Became Customers

Website/Blog/Podcast	Google	Trade Show	Referral	LinkedIn	Email	Twitter
21	6	6	4	3	2	1

Most of the people who eventually become customers made contact with us cited our Website/Blog/Podcast as the initial contact. It becomes problematic to separate out how they originally found our website – so this is problematic as well.

But a few customers actually DO cite LinkedIn or Twitter as they way they found us first.

Addendum – Problem Triage Process

The best way to resolve social media problems is to be proactive, rather than reactive. Here's our process for triaging potential problems.

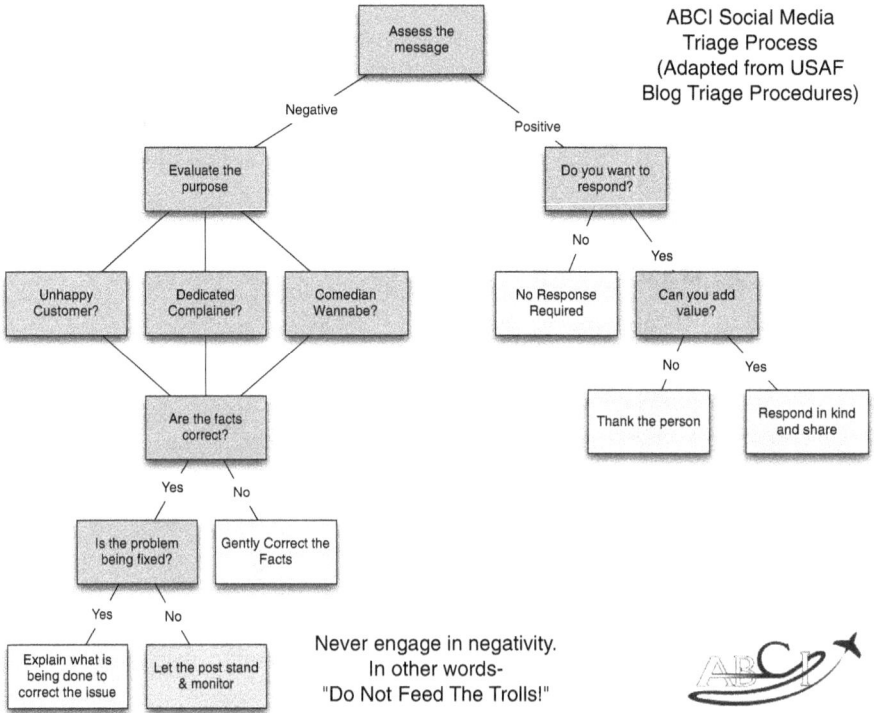

ABCI Social Media
Triage Process
(Adapted from USAF
Blog Triage Procedures)

Assess the message

Negative

Positive

Evaluate the purpose

Do you want to respond?

No

Yes

Unhappy Customer?

Dedicated Complainer?

Comedian Wannabe?

No Response Required

Can you add value?

No

Yes

Are the facts correct?

Thank the person

Respond in kind and share

Yes

No

Is the problem being fixed?

Gently Correct the Facts

Yes

No

Explain what is being done to correct the issue

Let the post stand & monitor

Never engage in negativity.
In other words-
"Do Not Feed The Trolls!"

Addendum – Hashtag Guide

"Twitter is the dumbest thing I've ever heard of."

Clearly, this man had heard that we do social media marketing for the aviation industry, and he intended to challenge me.

"I've heard of things that are much, much dumber." I said.

This was going to be fun. I didn't know if I could change his mind, but the small crowd that lingered after our presentation at an event was leaning in to hear what was going to happen next.

"Seriously, who wants to know what I had for breakfast? I think the whole idea is just really dumb." He said.

"I totally agree. Nobody wants to hear what you had for breakfast. " I heartily conceded.

I waited to see what he had to say next. Clearly he was curious, or he would not have started the conversation.

"So, what's the point?" He asked.

"What business are you in?" I asked him. (I know, it's rude to answer a question with a question, but I could see I had limited window, here.)

"My company makes avionics components." He said.

"So, there's a very specific group of people that need your product." I said.

"Exactly." He agreed.

"So, some of the things you need to do would be, keep up with who's talking about your products, who's talking about your competitors, what reporters for DOM and AIN and Avionics magazine are looking for, things like that?" I asked.

"Of course," He answered. "Which doesn't leave me much time for things like Twitter."

"Of course!" I responded. "So, what tools are you using to accomplish those things now?"

"Well, I read magazines and talk to people at trade shows like this one." He responded.

"Right. But did you know how many people are talking about 'avionics' on Twitter on the average day?"

"Not many." He said.

"Want to find out for sure?" I asked.

"Sure, why not." He conceded.

I whipped out my phone and browsed to hashtags.org and entered the term "avionics." I also added the words "avmro" (which I happened to know is a popular term with aviation maintenance people) and "aircraftmaintenance" for good measure. I showed him the screen, which looked something like this:

"Yeah, but who is it, and what are they saying?" He asked.

I quickly showed him how to search on a hashtag, (a fancy keyword) in Twitter.

Related searches

#jobs

Who to follow · Refresh · View all

Travel Blogger.com
Followed by ... and others
Follow

Chris
Follow

thomas marban
Follow

Find friends

Trends · Change

#McKinney
McKinney Police Pool Party Video: Officer Who Shoved, Handcuffed ...

#MyHour
Sir Bradley Wiggins breaks UCI Hour Record with distance of 54.526km

#TripleCrown
American Pharoah Wins Belmont Stakes and Triple Crown

#UCLFinal
Five moments that defined UCL final

#CanadianGP
Canadian GP: Lewis Hamilton leads home Nico Rosberg

Ivory Coast
Ivory Coast in turmoil ahead of start of Cup of Nations defence

MRI Placement Targeting 4

as seen
Buhari's inaugural speech: As seen by the world (1) - Vanguard News

Photos   View all

DWWTC
40 Must Have iPhone & iPad Apps in 2014 [AutonomousAvionics.com] #new #avionics #technology pinterest.com/pin/415175859...

Pinterest

iPad Resources
40 Must Have iPhone & iPad Apps in 2014 | AutonomousAvionics.com] #new #avionics #technology

View on web

PPT Search
NextGen Avionics Powerpoint Presentations - pptpunter.com/nextgen-avioni... #NextGen #Avionics

Neuvoo Springfield M
PDS Technical Services is looking for a «Avionics - Installer in «Springfield, apply now! #jobs neuvoo.com/job/job.php?id=zd3

"Avionics Magazine, Avidyne Corporation, Thales Group, ARINC Engineers, Runway Girl, and many, many others. And I can scroll through these pretty quickly and decide which are worth reading and which are not. "

"I didn't know you could put pictures in there." He admitted.

"So, if we agreed to call this 'competitive research' and 'ad targeting,' rather than Twitter and Topsy, would you use these tools?" I asked him.

"That would make me feel better about it." He said good-naturedly.

"Sounds good. You've got a deal." I said.

How to Use Hashtags

The term "hashtag" simply means a word or term preceded by the pound (or "hash" sign – #)

When you add a hashtag to a tweet or Instagram message attached to your update, photo or ad, that helps people who are looking for that specific topic to find it more easily by typing the term into the search window.

This list of aviation hashtags is not meant to be exhaustive, it's just to give you some ideas of how to begin your research and targeting for social media marketing.

It's often a good idea to include a very popular hashtag with a more specific one, so that you get the benefits of both.

When we complete a **Marketing Flight Plan** for our clients, we include a competitive analysis of what your top competitors are doing on social media, how large their audience is, and what their primary topics include.

Depending on the service level our clients choose, we take care of much of this research and targeting for them.

Here's a quick hashtag marketing guide to get you started. The statistics varies, but this report on original tweets (on Twitter) will give you a general idea of how popular these tags are. Tags generally have similar proportion on Instagram, Facebook and all other social media that use hashtags.

Aviation in General

Hashtag	Original Tweets in 24 hours
#aviation	811
#bizav	112
#airport	107
#airplane	66
#avion	34

"Geeks" who have specialized aviation knowledge

Hashtag	Tweets in the last 24 hours
#avgeek	112
#avnerd	10
#planegeek	6

For airline crews

Hashtag	Tweets in the last 24 hours
#crewlife	12
#pilotlife	11
#flightattendant	6
#cockpitview	4
#thisismyjob	43

Photography

Hashtag	Instagram posts in the last 24 hours
#aviationphotography	201
#instaplane	198
#planeporn	191
#skyporn	132

Flight Schools

Hashtag	Tweets in the last 24 hours
#flightschool	74
#timebuilding	6
#flightinstruction	2

Aircraft Maintenance & Ground Crews

Hashtag	Tweets in the last 24 hours
#aircraftmaintenance	165
#avmro	132
#ramplife	101
#avionics	99
#groundcrew	49

Aviation Trade Shows & Conventions

Aviation trade shows and conferences typically have their own hashtag so that exhibitors and attendees can stay informed about happenings at the event:

#nbaa20

#osh20

#sdc20

The easiest way to find the "official" event hashtag is to look at the event website, or watch for news from the organizing body. (NBAA, Aviation Week, Aviation Pros, etc.) They generally end in the year.

Action Items

Want to create your own hashtag? Go right ahead!
There's no central authority or governing body regulating their use.

Addendum 2- Aviation Digital Marketing Glossary

Aviation professionals understand the need for precise language. Aviation has more unique terms than just about any other profession! Digital marketing also has a specialized language.

Unfortunately, this can lead to misunderstandings, and even to unfortunate situations where aviation professionals purchase digital marketing services from slick service providers who don't take the time to be understood, and both parties end up frustrated and disappointed with the results.

This is sad because aviation sales marketing professionals stand to gain a lot from intelligent use of digital marketing!

In our practice, not a month goes by when someone tells us about being "taken for a ride" by a fast-talking digital marketing salesperson. This sort of thing is bad for everyone – it gives marketing companies a bad name, and causes aviation companies to waste valuable resource on services that aren't right for them or don't provide the results they expect.

This glossary isn't intended to make anyone a "native speaker" of digital marketing terminology, but hopefully we can prevent some unfortunate misunderstandings.

The difference between the almost-right word and the right word
is really a large matter –
'tis the difference between the lightening-bug and the lightening.

-Mark Twain

Term	Meaning
Boosted Post	Converting a Facebook post to a paid ad by "boosting" it, using a simple feature in Facebook to increase its visibility to a selected group of Facebook users that might not otherwise see it.
Bot	A program or "robot" that performs some function on the Internet, often scanning for specific words, images or files.
Chat bot	A program or "robot" that responds with text messages.
Company Page	Usually referring to Facebook or LinkedIn. People have individual profiles, but companies can also have "pages" which function somewhat like a profile. They represent the business or brand, rather than representing a specific person.
CPC	Cost Per Click. Can range from pennies per click to several dollars for the most competitive keywords.
CPM	Cost Per Thousand (Views.)
Crawler	AKA – a "bot," "robot," or "spider," specifically designed to search or scan for specific words, images or files.
Dark post	A social media paid post or advertisement, usually on Facebook, that is not visible from the company page timeline, but is intended only for a specific audience.
External Link	AKA "inbound link." A link to your website from a different site.
Facebook	Originally designed for college students to interact socially, now the largest social network.
Facebook Marketing	As the largest social network, Facebook offers the most granular and specific marketing options of any social media.
Friends	People who have requested and received a connection on Facebook. (These are called "connections" on LinkedIn and "followers" on Twitter.
Hashtag	Any word preceded by a pound sign, making it easy to find on some social media (particularly Twitter and Instagram)

Hyperlink	Usually simply called a "link," a clickable image or underlined word on a website or social media post.
IM	Instant messaging or online chat.
Image Tag	Words identifying an image. Usually not seen on the website but placed in the underlying code to help search engines and bots identify and index images.
Impression	Each time an ad is viewed in a browser on any device – desktop, tablet or phone. Note – it doesn't necessarily have to be clicked or acted upon to count as an impression.
Inbound Link	AKA "External Link." A link to your website from a different site.
Inbound Marketing	A strategy that focuses on attracting customers via company-related internet content and acquiring their contact information in exchange for high-value information.
Instant Messaging	A type of online chat – real-time text messages transmitted over the Internet.
Keyword Density	The number of times a keyword appears in a post.
Keywords	Words or phrases that capture the essence of a topic or document, used by search engines (Google, Yahoo, etc.) to find the most relevant material to people searching.
Landing Page	A page intended to be the first one viewed on a website. Could be the home page, but usually built for a specific purpose.
Lead Magnet	A mechanism on a website or social media encouraging people to subscribe to future updates (or marketing) in exchange for high-value information, such as a buyer's guide or tip sheet.
Link	AKA "hyperlink," a clickable image or underlined word on a website or social media post.
Link Farm	A site built specifically for the purpose of creating external links to boost search engine results for client sites. Often created as a directory or low-quality blog with many gratuitous links.
LinkedIn	Using the LinkedIn social media platform for marketing, either by searching for prospects based on specific criteria or by publishing paid ads to specific

Marketing	individuals.
LinkedIn Articles	Longer and more complex that LinkedIn Updates, the Articles function allows for a complex blog hosted on the LinkedIn social media platform.
LinkedIn Updates	Short, simple social media updates on the LinkedIn platform.
MeetEdgar	A social media posting and aggregating tool.
Messenger marketing	Using chat, IM or Facebook Messenger for marketing purposes, usually by broadcasting text messages and responding to text messages using a bot or computer program.
Meta tags	Meta tags are words and phrases attached to an item on the web, such as a web page or image (see "image tags") to help search engines and other bots to scan and index the material.
Organic Listings	Search engine results that are not paid ads.
Organic Results	See organic listings. Unpaid search engine results.
Outbound Marketing	Reaching out to prospects with direct mail, telephone, connecting on social media, usually unsolicited.
Paid Ad	An ad on any social media or search engine that has been paid for.
Paid Listing	A listing in any directory that was paid for.
Pay Per Click	Terms of sale of an online advertisement that include an agreement to pay a specific amount each time a link or image is clicked, presumably bringing visitors to your own website or product page.
Permission Marketing	AKA "Inbound Marketing."
Personal Page	AKA "Profile" on a social media channel. Personal pages with a minimum of information are required to log into Facebook and LinkedIn, where permissions are based on your personal account.
Podcast	Audio (or video) files, usually on a specific topic, usually a series with a subscription, hosted by iTunes, Stitcher, or Google Play. Popular aviation

	podcasts are hosted by Aviation Week, The Airplane Geeks, and others.
PPC	Pay Per Click
Profile	AKA "Personal Page" on a social media channel. Personal pages with a minimum of information are required to log into Facebook and LinkedIn, where permissions are based on your personal account.
Rankings	Where your site or page appears in the search results, AKA "search results" aka "search page" aka "SERP." The first five spaces or the first page of results is the most coveted because most Internet searchers usually don't search past the first page of results.
Redirect	Code that causes a visitor to find himself on a different web page. Often used as a shortcut for convenience or marketing. For example, if you type in ABCI1.com you will be redirected to AviationBusinessConsultants.com.
Results Page	AKA "search results" aka "search page" aka "SERP." The page that appears after you type a specific keyword or phrase into a search engine. The first five spaces or the first page of results is the most coveted because most Internet searchers usually don't search past the first page of results.
Robot	A program or "bot" that performs some function on the Internet, often scanning for specific words, images or files.
ROI	Return on Investment. One way to calculate a return on investment for digital marketing is to review sales made during the year,
RSS	Real Simple Syndication – Usually used to re-use content on your website to another location. (To automatically publish to a podcast or social media feed, for example.)
Search Engine	Google, Bing, Yahoo, etc. A web page that web visitors use to search for pages, videos or images on a particular topic, using "search terms" AKA "keywords."
Search Term	AKA "keyword"
SEM	Search engine marketing. Techniques used to make your content show up more prominently in search results. Includes paid search options like Pay Per Click ads, optimizing content for better organic search results, (SEO) and adding more content to attract the attention of the search engines.
SEO	Search Engine Optimization. Visible and invisible changes made to a website, web pages, images, and other parts of a website to make it easier for the

	search engines to find and index. This helps visitors using search engines to find your website more easily.
SEO Audit	An evaluation of your website to find ways to make it perform better search engines. The starting point of any good Search Engine Optimization program.
SERP	Search Engine Results Page. The page that pops up when people search for a particular keyword.
Sitemap	An outline of the pages on your website, designed to help people or (more often) search engines find their way around your site. An XML sitemap is built in a programming language and is intended for search engines.
SlideShare	Owned by LinkedIn, a social media network designed to help people share and find slide presentations on specific topics. Can be used to explain topics or even sell products.
Social Media	Any website or app that helps people interact with one another. The most popular social media networks for aviation industry professionals are LinkedIn, Facebook, Twitte Slideshare and a few others.
Social Network	See Social Media. Could also be used to describe all of your connections on a particular social media platform or across all platforms. (ABCI's company page has a social network of 5,200 on Facebook, I'm personally connected with 2,785 on Linkedin.)
Spider	AKA – a "bot," "robot," or "crawler," specifically designed to search or scan for specific words, images or files.
Subscribe	A key component of inbound marketing. When a person "friends," "likes" or "follows" you on a social media platform, they are essentially subscribing to see updates from you in the future. You can also set up "lead magnets" on your website inviting visitors to subscribe, usually in exchange for some high-value information they want.
Tweet	A post or update on Twitter.
Tweetup	A meeting where people who are connected on social media (usually Twitter) meet. There are often Tweetups for social media connections at major aviation conventions.
Twitter	A social media platform that emphasizes short updates. (Twitter.com)
Twitter	Posts on Twitter designed to advertise a product or service.

Marketing	
UGC	User-Generated Content. When you enable comments on a blog post or run a photo contest, you are asking your website visitors or social media connections to submit "User Generated Content." Social media is almost entirely composed of UGC.
Usability Audit	An audit of your website based on industry-standard practices. For example, most people look for a search or shopping cart function in the upper right corner, and most people look for underlined links. A Usability Audit evaluates how well the website conforms to these conventions.
User Generated Content	AKA "UGC" – When you enable comments on a blog post or run a photo contest, you are asking your website visitors or social media connections to submit "User Generated Content." Social media is almost entirely composed of UGC.
Viral Marketing	Content created with the intention of being shared on social media. "Viral" is meant to describe how a virus moves from one organism to another. But in digital marketing, the "virality" of a post is based on how many people share it with their own social networks.
Web 2.0	Web 2.0 does not refer to an update to any technical specification, but to changes in the way Web pages are designed and used. A Web 2.0 website may allow users to interact and collaborate with each other in a social media dialogue as creators of user-generated content in a virtual community, in contrast to the first generation of Web 1.0-era websites where people were limited to the passive viewing of content. Examples of Web 2.0 features include social networking sites and social media sites (e.g., Facebook), blogs, wikis, folksonomies ("tagging" keywords on websites and links), video sharing sites (e.g., YouTube), hosted services, Web applications ("apps"), collaborative consumption platforms, and mashup applications.
Web Conference	AKA "Webinar" – A seminar delivered over the Internet, so that participants can hear audio and see video or slides, and usually participate by asking questions via a chat function.
Webinar	AKA "Web Conference" – A seminar delivered over the Internet, so that participants can hear audio and see video or slides, and usually participate by asking questions via a chat function.

Website Audit	Website Audits can be based on Search Engine Optimization (to improve the number of visitors) or Usability (to help turn those visitors into customers, clients, passengers, etc. The intention is to improve the marketing performance of a website.
Wiki	A website that allows collaborative editing of its content by users.
Wikipedia	The world's largest wiki, an online user-generated encyclopedia. People and things can be submitted for inclusion into Wikipedia and are confirmed by a board of volunteer editors who enforce a set of guidelines. It can be a great marketing strategy to create a Wikipedia entry.
XMP Sitemap	AKA "sitemap." An outline of the pages on your website, designed to help search engines find their way around your site.
YouTube	A social media platform where participants view or submit videos.

Addendum 3 - Social Media Habits of Highly Effective Salespeople

With a hat tip to Stephen Covey, this was just a bit ahead of his time!

This is how I fit social media into my sales cadence. Professional sales folks – how do YOU use social media effectively for the amount of time you spend?

And, out of curiosity – how much time do you spend?

It's called Social Media for a reason, right?

Here's my recipe for interacting on social media:

LinkedIn

- Three connections

- Three thoughtful comments

This is in addition to the fairly canned "Happy Birthday" and "Congratulations" that the app suggests.

Facebook

- Visit Three Company Pages

- Three Likes

- Three Comments

Twitter

- Review Three Hashtags

- Three Replies

- Three Retweets

Total – about 45 minutes.

I do this routine (or part of it) every time I'm trapped in the car, plane or train, or waiting for something and don't have another immediate, interruptable task available.

Other Resources

Is The Marketing Lab for You?

Insider's Circle is our "tribe" of current clients. We're lucky enough to work with people who care about the Aviation industry and about each other! So, we've provided a set of resources to help our Insiders help themselves and each other.

Insider Circle Mission: To help aviation industry professionals achieve success by selling more of their products and services, and to become the leader of their respective niche or specialty.

- Help you dominate in your niche of Aviation by supplying the best content, techniques, and skills in Aviation sales and marketing.

- Provide unparalleled networking and connections with the most influential people in the industry.

- Supply branded and co-branded products to increase your customer base and greatly increase your sales.

- Provide outstanding value to every member so that for every minute or dollar you invest in the Insider Circle you get your investment back ten-fold.

The Insider's Circle is not for everybody. In fact, we anticipate only 1% of the sales and marketing professionals in the Aviation Industry will ever be part of this group!

The Marketing Insiders' Manifesto:

To sum up ABCI's marketing philosophy, which comes from our years of experience working with small businesses, Fortune 50 businesses, and aviation companies of all stripes:

1. No "Random Acts of Marketing."

2. Everything must be part of a system, with an input and an output.

3. Every campaign must have a list, an offer (or CTA), and presentation.

4. Every qualified prospect must have interest, resources and authority to make a purchase.

5. Habits matter more than massive effort.

6. Marketing doesn't have to be pretty or perfect, but it DOES have to be effective.

7. Diversity = Stability.

8. Marketing awards don't sell products.

9. Never invent what you can adapt.

10. Simplify your message!

Final Word

Thank you for spending time with our book. We truly believe that better business practices and better marketing improve the industry and a healthy aviation industry is better for everyone!

We do two pro-bono marketing projects and offer two scholarships per year for our Marketing Lab.   Contact us for an application!

If you have questions, comments, or would like to talk with us about just about anything aviation-related, we do free consultations on a limited basis.   Visit our web site for details. AviationbusinessConsultants.com

Aviation iis a small world, so if you see us at a convention or trade show, please don't be shy – introduce yourself!

www.ingramcontent.com/pod-product-compliance
Lightning Source LLC
Chambersburg PA
CBHW070926210326
41520CB00021B/6820